THE EXTINCTION CLUB

THE EXTINCTION CLUB

Robert Twigger

wm

WILLIAM MORROW
An Imprint of HarperCollins*Publishers*

for samia

ACKNOWLEDGMENTS

It is necessary to thank first all those without whom this book could not have been written, including the following: the Marquess and Marchioness of Tavistock; Lavinia; Callum, for his patience and help, and all the staff who took the time to be of service at Woburn Abbey; Lord Andrew Howland, for unfailing hospitality and assistance; Klaudia, though I'm sorry it didn't quite work out as planned; Andrew Kidd, for the considerable faith and vision to take the project on; Brigitte, of course, and Stephanie Cabot, for the sudden inspiration and constant support; in China: Dr. Ho Lee Fuk and Mr. Wang Fu Dong; in France: Dr. J. Rushbrooke, for invaluable research assistance, and Mme. C. David, for wise advice.

To claim that it is true is nowadays the convention of every made-up story.
Mine, however, is true.
—JORGE LUIS BORGES, *The Book of Sand*

It is easier to gain than to secure the advantages of victory.
—CHINESE PROVERB

THE EXTINCTION CLUB

MAJOR

JOHN MAJOR III's disabled foot flopped this way and that as he got into the front seat of the Chrysler four-wheel drive vehicle. I had to admit that for a millionaire he was careless of his appearance. His shoes were cheap slip-ons. To get around he used a hospital-issue green canvas wheelchair. When I remarked on his name, as every Englishman must, he didn't show much more reaction than a wheezy grin as he reached for another Kent menthol cigarette. Inexplicably, he had ripped the filters off some, as if he was smoking Kents under sufferance. He was ill, but he was rich, and being rich is most important if you want to be a Big Game Hunter.

All of us were now in the Chrysler, heading out to the Kill Zone. That's what I called it to myself. The others, Tom the guide and John Major III, called it "the stalk."

We were driving fast down a dusty road in Texas in the cold December dawn to kill a deer. But this was no ordinary deer. John Major III didn't mind telling me that it was costing him five thousand dollars to shoot a young buck he wouldn't normally look twice at. The deer we were after was a Pere David, an animal so rare, or endangered if you prefer, that it is extinct in the wild, and has been for the last one thousand years. The Chinese call it Milu.

The plan was to drive slowly up to a clump of trees near to the place where the Pere Davids gathered in the early morning. John Major would then take his shot from his seated position in the front of the Chrysler, his gun poking through the open window and resting on the outsize wing mirror.

Tom the guide, who wore Realtree Advantage camo gear and yellow-tinted dark glasses, had told me earlier that some shooters preferred the car shot to a more realistic sneaking-up shot. "They're here for the rack, don't matter how they get it," opined Tom. The rack was the head of antlers on the deer.

Tom also took people lion-hunting on the Texas ranch. "Got to keep the deer away from the lions, though," he said with a smile. He told me how the lions spent most of their time in a small compound before being shot in a slightly larger compound.

The advantage of shooting Pere Davids was that there was no "natural" precedent to influence the "romance" of the kill. Every Pere David killed since guns were invented has been shot in a game park of some sort.

John Major's gun was a new acquisition, a .308 B. S. Johnson Special with a new-fangled plastic stock, fold-up bipod, and "several other interesting features." He told me that he had many guns, and believed gun-collecting was almost as great a pleasure as acquiring trophy heads.

"But what about the actual killing?" I asked.

"The moment of death? That's neither pleasure nor displeasure," he said. "It's going to sound strange, I guess, but I think of it as a lovin' duty."

Tom eased off the dirt road and onto the worn-down grass of the range. The trees we were heading for were actually a clump of high bushes with straight, bare branches. Tom put the vehicle into the lowest gear and we trickled over the range with a bumpy rumble.

John Major III looked keenly out of the window at the standing and grazing forms just beyond the clump of bushes. There were five or six, all males, not one older than two years. "Spikers," as Tom called them, their antlers just single prongs, with no branching spikes or "points."

"That one," said Tom after looking through his glasses. Zeiss 7×50s, just like the ones used by the hero in *For Whom the Bell Tolls*. John Major III had Zeisses too, but a more compact version, newer. Tom took a lot of care in showing which deer John Major was to shoot. It was slightly away from the herd, head down and grazing. It seemed to me to have a large patch of mange on its side, but I thought it prudent to keep my voice down as I was, after all, only a limey, and an unarmed one at that.

John Major III took several hand-loaded cartridges and fed them into the breech using the bolt to suck them in. He always hand-loaded his ammo because "at five grand a pop I don't want factory ammo going off wild."

The vehicle was silent now, engine off, parked in half shade behind the tall bushes. The breeze was cool when John Major wound the window right down. The gun barrel sneaked onto the wing mirror strut. John Major put his fat cheek to the stock and squinted down the telescopic sights, his trigger finger already curled into position. At the last minute he pushed his ear protectors down into position. Tom did too. Mine had been down for a while—I'd been caught out before by a .308 cartridge in a confined space and it had been deafening. I looked out at the deer— long tail, thick neck, two points of antlers—certainly it did not seem to sense death. Then I looked at the trigger finger, seeing if I could see it move. John Major's wheezing was the loudest thing in the car until BANG.

BANG. There is no gun, no guide, no "me," certainly not one that's been to Texas to shoot exotic deer. Sorry, Klaudia, I know I told you I'd been there and done that, but it just wasn't true. There's no John Major III—though I was beginning to like him. There's no Chrysler 4 WD (do they make such a vehicle?), and there is no deer, emphatically no dead deer. It's all made up. Lies. Farrago of. Tissue of. Lies. Damned lies. Not Not Not true. Never was.

Now comes the tricky part. Why? Why do it? Why lie?

More to the point, why couldn't I keep going? Why stop after three pages?

All I can say is that this story is better true than made up. I realize that now. And knowing this has had an effect. Destroyed my morale. That's why I had to give up. Fuck it. I've got to tell the truth. There's nothing else for it, nothing else I can do, not now, not after making a false start of my "false" start. The truth.

In reality I'm sitting on the seventh-floor rooftop garden of my in-laws in Egypt. The garden is dusty, with a pruned kind of Astroturf underfoot, like the ponds of green furze used to signify grass on a model train set. The view is dusty and distant, as far as the sandstone cliffs at the edge of the city where the rubbish of twenty million people gets picked over and burned. Before the cliffs there are shell-like mini tower blocks, gray concrete apartment blocks, and big villas with rubble on their roofs. All over Cairo, whatever direction you look in, you will see piles of rubble on people's roofs. Some of the rubble is obviously from the house concerned, but some seems strangely out of place, as if the owner has dumped the rubble there just to fit in.

And of course the satellite dishes—huge ones for the rich, medium-sized ones for the middle classes, and tiny little dusty hubcaps stuck everywhere for the teeming poor, bristling everywhere, all patinated with the same dust as the rubble, all of a piece and looking somehow ancient, under the hot dust haze of the day.

I am in Cairo to write this book. My excuse is that I just couldn't do it in England. My son, who is only five months old, just wouldn't let me. In Cairo there are many people who want to look after him, so my wife and I came here to escape the torture of being two isolated adults with a baby in a small house, without even a job to escape to.

In Cairo, surrounded by dust, noise, and pollution, I can relax. And get this book done.

TRUTH

A ZOIC ROCK, crumbling, cracked, and expanded by rare earth in exposed strata, the earth powdery and blowing up now and all morning into the faces of the Han poor, thin-chested old Chinamen conscripted to dig holes for the foreign man whose khaki shirt stretched over his important belly. Herbert Boileau. Boileau—self-styled professor, sometime photographer for *National Geographic*, a veteran of the Lafayette Brigade of the Great War (as he always referred to it), an American who affected Britishness in order to impress. If this did not sufficiently engage, he would inspissate his talk with Latin and the odd dialect word of Wei Chinese, allowing the strange, elongated sounds to hang in the air like a challenge.

Boileau roughly tolerated his competitors in the field of Chinese paleontology, Father Teilhard de Chardin and Arthur Sowerby of Shanghai. Boileau spent more time in the field than either, had neither de Chardin's penchant for mysticism nor Sowerby's preference for dull fact over extravagant theory. That he was a liar had not, so far, impeded his rapid progress, now set on Sinitic archaeology after failed ventures in pharmacology and railway-line surveying. If questioned about exactly which professorial chair he held, Emeritus was uttered with sufficient force to stop casual prying. That he had faked no discovery pleased him: Chinese earth was rich enough to provide without recourse to Hong's antiquaries shop in Peking. His reports were a different matter. Here Boileau knew that a good story should prevail. He admired Schliemann over Pitt-Rivers for the German millionaire's appreciation of narrative. If there was a Troy to uncover in the Ch'ien T'ang estuaries of the south, Herbert Boileau would be the man to do it.

The day was cold, with a constant dry wind picking up earth from the diggings, whipping dust from the huge man-high wheelbarrows pushed and maneuvered by sunburned Chinese paid by the tightfisted Boileau in clipped silver taels and opium, men who would tolerate breathing the mica-laden rare earth that made every man's hair bright orange by the day's end. Boileau's only rule was not to reemploy men who turned up with earth on their faces the following day. Men so careless of their own appearance might break something valuable.

Toiling in the pits were the younger men, paid more, with a tobacco allowance as well as opium and silver. Paid more, but not resented by the older wrecked shells of men working the heavy barrows.

The men were younger, but few of them were whole. Many lacked several fingers on each hand. Those using the light brushes were all one-handed persistent thieves who had escaped south from the Muslim territories of Kansu. Boileau knew they were thieves, but thieves have sharp eyes—and at the day's end they were all made to file unclothed through an outhouse of upright logs and flapping muddy canvas.

Boileau needed every man he could get because of the curse attendant upon the great square holes he insisted on digging. The site was not propitious—a rammed-earth plateau bounded by stunted ginkgo trees, a Shang-dynasty burial site still avoided as a place of the dead. It lay on a bluff over a fork in the river, the bones washed up on the foreshore taken by most locals to mean that the whole area was a reliquary, a place of ghosts and the white birds that always accompany ghosts.

Earth spumed off a perfect cone of tipped dirt. Boileau was reminded of one season in Japan and seeing the snow fly off the tip of Mount Fuji, but white, not dark orange. Each night, in the run-down shuttered lodgings of the headman, Boileau called for a lacquered basin of water, cold as they could make it, to sluice out the orange dirt from his nostrils. Half the time he'd wear a yellow silk triangle over his face, but it was always dropping and had to be removed when he needed a pipe. And even his pipe stem tasted of earth.

It was 4:30 P.M., the half just struck on Boileau's hunter, a timepiece cased in gunmetal that rang each quarter hour and nestled under his rubberized-cloth ulster in one voluminous pocket. The hunter had been through his year of the Great War, the chiming deactivated by a watchmaker in Charlesroi, and after the war was made to ring more loudly, announcing the presence of Boileau, no longer under orders, a free man at last.

The half hour had rung and Boileau was already feeling under his ulster for the briar, prefilled with a mixture of imported latakia and local tobacco. A huge sieve, secured by three ropes to a rough wooden davit, trailed earth as it was lifted. As it went up in two jerky moves the men below cheered, in the curiously musical yet muted fashion they favored, men whistling for the wind through broken teeth.

In the sieve were the dirt-encrusted flat parts of two deer's antlers. Flat blades with a knuckle pattern at one end. Boileau had seen grave-site antlers before; indeed it was he who had first suggested they were *Elaphurus davidianus*, Pere David's deer, rather than the spurious *Rucervus menziesanus* claimed by the Reverend James Menzies.

The three-fingered man who swung the davit was pointing repeatedly, stabbing his first finger, the middle one, again and again at the sieve. The pipe could wait. Boileau trod carefully around the duckboarded top of the ten-foot-deep hole. He brushed the man away as he tried to hand over the flat antler piece. Boileau picked it out himself, seeing at once the deep engravings that covered the thing—not Chinese characters but pictograms recognizably from the Shang dynasty; he'd seen them on mortuary bronzes and deer scapulae excavated in Tsi-nan Fu,

Shantung province. The scapulae, always from Pere David's deer, were used as writing tablets for the so-far-indecipherable pictographic Shang script.

To scry the future was another use for the deer bones and antler blades. Turtle plastrons were also used. The bone was drilled into and then a red-hot piece of metal was briefly inserted. The resulting T-shaped stress crack was interpreted as lucky or unlucky. Some of these divinatory objects were also inscribed with pictograms.

Boileau deliberately slowed his actions, sensing the victory that was soon to be his, as he blew the fine integumental earth from the second antler. Pictograms and, underneath them, recognizable early Chinese characters. A bilingual document, not quite a Rosetta stone but still the first of its kind in China. At last he could translate from the prehistoric past.

All this earth, and the Chinamen around grinning fit to burst, knowing that this was good for them too. Boileau holding up the antlers to the weak distant coin of the sun, hidden behind haze. Now he had something. Now he really had something.

He looked around his crew of grinning misfits. One old man in mud-caked sandals was laughing, his whole locked frame rocking forward and backward. Boileau saw the arcus senilis, canescent eyes, a narrow band of white that ringed the old man's irises, long thought to be a portent.

Months later, the first translated antler of *Elaphurus davidianus* told of a ten-day week, of dreams and sacrifices and the fortunes of the hunt. There was no similarity between most pictograms—which looked like runes or a game of hangman—and the angular early Ku-Wen script. One ideograph, though, had hardly changed from its pictorial origin: the symbol for man and the symbol for word, which when combined read then and still read now as *true, sincere, truth.*

TRUTH II

I REMEMBER THE experience very clearly, even though it was several years ago. I was attempting to write a book in a cramped flat in London, and every sentence I typed seemed to be mired in bullshit, hitting all the wrong notes, useless. I looked out of the window despairingly and saw a sparrow perched on a tree branch, the wind ruffling his gray belly feathers making him look fatter than he really was. The sparrow is a rare creature now—it has suffered an incredible 92 percent decline in the last ten years. Kensington Gardens was home to 2,603 sparrows in 1925, 544 in 1975, but only 48 in 1995. And in the last five years that number has dropped to 12.

But that day I wasn't looking at the sparrow as a sad reminder that we've cocked things up in the world; I was grateful for this fellow creature as an antidote to what I was writing.

Somehow the bird seemed like truth.

And what I was writing seemed vaguely false.

That isn't always the case. Especially with poetry; it's what we strive for there, that spot-on feeling. Life is closer to poetry than prose.

Spot on, in focus, somehow bracing. I looked at the bird and felt by looking that it brought me back to earth, back to reality, provided that truth feeling. The bird could not be vaguely false. The bird was true, provided the truth feeling.

The wild animal, the mountain covered in flowers, the summer river—all these things are in focus if we care to look in the right way, if we can remain a little *surprised* by what we are looking at.

I'm sure this is one reason why we like looking at wild animals. Their survival guarantees an intangible resource of truth.

And it seems to work best with wild animals—wild birds, or rare deer like Milu. Pigs and cows and chickens don't seem to work as well.

THE PHONE CALL

IT WAS in the same cramped flat as the above that I received the phone call. I'm in my mid-thirties and my wife is expecting our first child and I'm writing but earning no money when out of the blue the phone call comes. I'd been fantasizing about this phone call for ten years, ever since my final year at university. THE PHONE CALL that will CHANGE YOUR LIFE WITH MONEY. The phone call that happens to other people, usually in implausible movies. The phone call. I'd begun to doubt that it would ever happen; in fact,

I dated my modest success in the last few years to the moment when I ceased believing in the phone call's existence.

My wife worked while I exercised my right to be poor. I'd written books, but it would be an error to say that I'd written them for money. My daily bread came from a variety of other sources, including teaching grammar to a Hong Kong millionaire's son called Vincent Ho.

Vincent was difficult to like. He had the hairless body of an alien and a barely concealed contempt for his Oxford-educated grammar tutor. Sometimes he would make me accompany him to the cashpoint for my wages. He'd casually draw out five hundred pounds and hand me a tenner, pocketing the rest in his designer hipsters as he headed toward Soho.

I picked up the phone. It was my agent, my American agent. Her name is Brigitte. Even though I had earned her almost less than she had paid out on lunch for me, she had never lost faith in me. That kind of loyalty is very heartwarming. She's an American, and Americans are both my favorite and most hated people. Brigitte was calling me from a mobile phone, it was that urgent.

BRIGITTE: I have just heard the most amazing story in the world.
ME: Great!
BRIGITTE: I was at lunch with Andrew Howland—Lord Andrew Howland—you know, he runs Woburn, the safari park?
ME: Oh, yes, I went there last year. (True, we went there after discovering Windsor Safari Park had closed and become Legoland, in order to satisfy an inexplicable urge to visit a safari park. Any safari park will do in such a case.)

BRIGITTE: Andrew Howland told me that he has these amazing deer called Pere David's deer, because they were saved from extinction in China by a guy called Pere David at the time of the Boxer Rebellion.

ME: A fascinating time in Chinese history. In fact, my great-grandfather fought there. (OK, he was there—whether he fought or not I didn't know.)

BRIGITTE: It gets even better. Andrew Howland's great-great-grandfather, the Duke of Bedford, brought these deer back to Woburn and bred them and they thrived, but the ones in China all died out. So his great-great-grandfather saved the species. And they returned some deer to China a few years back—isn't that amazing?

At this point I thought the story was OK, but not amazing. Brigitte then told me how much she could sell the story for, if it was done in the right way. It was a five-figure sum equivalent to about twenty years of teaching grammar to reluctant Chinese millionaires. . . .

(Huge, mind-blowing mental pause that lasts no time in real time but acts on my avaricious, cash-starved brain like sunlight and makes the story suddenly incredibly interesting.)

ME: Actually it *is* a pretty amazing story. Are you sure?

BRIGITTE: I just left the London Book Fair. I did a deal for a book about the history of racing pigeons for [a sum still huge but lower than our target]. Our story is better.

Already *our* story.

ME: You know, it's just struck me, the Boxer Rebellion was a fascinating period in history.

BRIGITTE: Precisely. The story has everything—China, the Boxer Rebellion, your great-grandfather, an English lord, deer. . . .

BRIGITTE AND ME TOGETHER: It's Bambi with history! It can't fail. (Sound of mental champagne corks popping.)

ME: X grand?

BRIGITTE: Maybe more, with foreign rights.

Foreign rights!

MY STORY

BRIGITTE'S MASTER plan started with me writing a blistering proposal. That wouldn't be too difficult. She told me she'd arrange for me to meet Lord Andrew Howland, the great-great-grandson of Herbrand Russell, the man who had saved the deer at Woburn. I looked forward to that, since I was not on familiar terms with any aristocrats, and somehow that felt like an omission in my life.

At this point I felt very positive about the whole thing. It wasn't just the money—though that couldn't be ignored—it was the challenge, the opportunity to write something historical, researched, authoritative, almost academic—but with literary knobs on, and best of all without *me* in it. My previous two books had been deeply autobiographical. Some readers had even complained that the word *I* had appeared too many times on each page. I did my best to rewrite *I* sentences without the *I*, but sometimes it just wasn't possible. Self-reference was part of the package.

Meanwhile, I rushed out and celebrated my soon-to-be-had wealth, my entry ticket to consumer normality: I bought a Leatherman Wave (which is the most expensive multitool in the world); a boxed collection of CDs by Herbie Hancock, a new mountain bike with suspension and huge pedals, the complete *The Man Without Qualities* by Robert Musil, a £120 trolley of food from Sainsbury's, and, my greatest folly, a secondhand sailing cruiser for seven hundred pounds.

EMPEROR

IN 1598, to tempt the Emperor of China to convert to Christianity, Matteo Ricci brought with him:

Paintings of Christ and John the Baptist
A breviary with gold-thread binding
A cross inlaid with precious stones
Pieces of polychrome glass containing relics of the saints
An atlas—the *Theatrum Orbis Terrarum* of Ortelius

A large clock with weights
A small striking clock of gilded metal worked by springs
Two prisms
A clavichord
Eight mirrors and bottles of different sizes
A rhinoceros tusk
Two sand clocks
The Four Gospels translated into Chinese
Four European belts
Five bolts of colored linen
Four cruzados.

Ricci had already been nearly ten years in China. His list of presents had to balance that which he thought worthy against that which he knew the emperor craved. Prisms were good—excellent, in fact, for giving away to high officials. The emperor would love a prism. But a piece of glass, however clever, requires no maintenance. A clock needs to be wound every day and can easily stop working if it is not cleaned and oiled. In the streets of Peking it was customary to wear a black veil against the insidious street dust that rose everywhere in great clouds. Ricci hoped the dust might even get into his clock, as it sat ticking in the contented emperor's throne room. If he were asked to mend the clock, he might have a chance to meet and talk with the emperor.

Ricci had taken pains to establish his reputation as an educated man. At first he had dressed as a non-Buddhist bonze, a priest. But bonzes have little status in China. He then styled himself as a graduate, exchanging coarse gray rags for a purple robe with a pale-blue border. Whenever he went outdoors he no longer walked but traveled by sedan chair, with a servant trotting behind him carrying copies of his twelve-page visiting book, forerunner of the business card.

Instead of sporting the bonze's shaven head, he now wore his hair shoulder length, with a beard finer than any mandarin. He did not prostrate himself in front of other scholars. At last the graduate classes of China could listen to him without shame.

When he entered the observatory in Nanking, he was able to show the embarrassed eunuchs that the Arab-designed torquetum, an instrument for measuring the position of the stars, was off by three and a half degrees. After it had been moved from Pingyang a century before, no one had thought to adjust it.

But it had been Ricci's memory, rather than his learning, that had most impressed the Chinese. He used the Jesuit method of holding an entire page, of the language to be learned, in the mind's eye as a basic reference and linking new words to be remembered to sentences on that page. Memorizing five hundred Chinese characters at one reading was not difficult for this strange scholar from a foreign land. For a country where advancement meant remembering the classics, this was a great gift indeed.

As his reputation grew, Ricci at last gained permission to visit Peking.

The emperor had seen no one face-to-face, apart from his eunuchs and concubines, for sixteen years.

Sometimes he watched people from behind a slatted blind on a balcony above the dragon throne. On such occasions, he would hold a tablet made of precious stones to his face, to inhibit the uptake of air breathed out by his guests.

Likewise, any visitor wanting to pay homage to the emperor was constrained by formality to hold an ivory tablet, three inches by eight inches, over the mouth when speaking so that the breath did not carry.

The grand eunuch informed Matteo Ricci that he would appear before the emperor in the company of Muslim traders from Kashgar. These men brought jade for the emperor, which was worked with quartz sand as an abrasive. Their main source of profit was buying rhubarb in Kansu, where it grew abundantly, and selling it dear in Peking, where it did not. But at the last minute the emperor chose not to appear.

Ricci never did meet the emperor, despite his present of the striking clock. His role as winder and mender of this clock ensured his close contact with the palace, but the eunuchs cleverly kept him from the celestial ruler Wan Li.

Everywhere in the Forbidden City Ricci saw the dragon guardian of the Middle Kingdom, a benevolent beast associated with life-giving rain, having a camel's head, a deer's antlers, a hare's eyes, a bull's ears, a snake's neck, a carp's scales, an eagle's five claws, and a tiger's paws.

LIBRARY

At this early stage I did all my research in the London Library. Until quite recently it had been possible to sneak into the library, which is the largest private library in the world, without being a member. But now there was a locked door, which could only be opened by a security guard behind a glass window. The security guard, along with the porters and other library menials, was wearing a silly red T-shirt with London Library written on it. This was just one of many blows to the old-world charm of the London Library, which I had been sneaking into, on and off, for the last ten years.

In that period, between 1989 and 1999, more things changed or got swept away than in the previous hundred years. To clarify this absurd-seeming statement, I should say, more of the things I thought of as belonging to a previous era got swept away. Things that had survived two world wars, nationalization, and Margaret Thatcher got swept away. This is what I felt, and it's connected to what I call the I've-always-arrived-too-late scenario. Japan was uniquely different pre-1985; I arrived in 1992. Borneo still had tribes that didn't use money in 1986; by 1996, when I arrived, money was all too familiar. Egypt in the 1980s was a place still touched by the mysteries of the past; by 1993, it was just starting to be choked to death by cars bought with profits made from the new global economy.

This is my own personal ax to grind. If it connects at all with the London Library, it is with the palpable modernization of an institution that had remained almost unchanged for a hundred years. And now that the T-shirts and security men were installed, it seemed, yet again, that I had arrived too late.

The library is popular because it has a huge collection of old books all on open-access stacks. The stacks are dark shelves of books in a cavernous, windowless shell of a building divided into seven floors. Each floor is made of thick cast iron with holes in it, and it's possible to see through each floor to the next. Just being there is enough to make you fantasize about shooting a film with a gun battle between the floors in the stacks; after all, theoretically, you could assassinate a reader on the seventh floor (say, one of the famous authors, such as A. S. Byatt, who frequent the place) by aiming carefully from the basement, which houses topography—my favorite section.

After the attraction of the stacks, with their thousands of ancient, yellowing books in leather covers, comes the reading room, with its leather-topped wooden tables and leather arm-chairs. As a place for sleeping off a heavy lunch it is unparalleled, though there is a stern-looking librarian who sits with a Silence sign on his desk. Which, of course, just adds to the charm of the place.

In the days before the security guard, the only concession to the twentieth century was a card-index system started in 1963. Before that, all acquisitions were entered into huge leather indexes. Card indexes are good if you are unfamiliar with the LL system (which you still should use for very early books), but once the complexities of the LL system are mastered, then it is extremely precise, rewarding, and quick. But until you master it, it seems illogical, chaotic, and slow.

After the card-index introduction came computerization. This led to the ability to practice covert surveillance on the members of the library, generally either wealthy Londoners, writers, or people who valued the old-fashioned nature of the reading room.

Introducing computers was a nasty turning point. One of the previous attractions of the place was that the staff *never* told you off. Because there was no cumulative record of books borrowed, they could never, at the point of borrowing, give you a stern lecture on fines and returning books on time. In fact, there were *no* fines. But once the computers arrived, they could keep a better eye on their—how do they think of us?—customers.

Admittedly, it was remarkably easy to steal books from the old London Library. And it was one of those peculiar moments in life, felt to be salutary in some way, a mixture of sadness and exasperation, when, after a long search, one had to conclude that *Wanderings in West Africa* by Winwood Reade (1865) had been nicked.

Add together security guards, men in red T-shirts, computers, a proposed tearoom (postponed for the time being), and surveillance, and the old, classy, clubland LL seems a long way away.

Because it was impossible to sneak in anymore, I had to become a "member." This cost £120. Being a member, however, made me feel proprietorial and therefore more entitled to feel upset by the changes. More upset than I'd felt before. I decided the staff of the LL thought it was being run for their benefit. It was the library equivalent of restaurants where all the waiters hang around at the bar having a great time while the customers get annoyed. Eventually such places go bust, I fumed to myself.

It was thinking thoughts like these that drew me to the simple photocopied flyer that was mysteriously inserted into the book on my desk in the reading room while I was downstairs using the magnificent Victorian toilets in the basement. The flyer invited me to a meeting of readers disturbed by recent developments at the London Library. I had discovered the League against (modernizing) the London Library. I liked the way *modernizing* was in parentheses. The L(m)LL. My kind of league.

ISBN ENVY

I SCANNED A lot of books, which in my case meant holding the book, flipping through it, and not reading a word except the date it was published and any author info, especially the age of the author (a) now and (b) when he wrote the book, how many books in total the author had written, and any exciting things he had done, such as fighting in wars or living abroad. Increasingly I felt under pressure from authors who had published large numbers of books. I preferred authors who didn't start writing until their fifties; that gave me more scope for catching up. Writers who had exciting lives gave me cause for contemplating whether my own life was exciting enough. The ones who had a steady stream of publications dating from their early twenties made me start calculating on fingers and thumbs how many books a year I'd have to write to catch them up. Reading about other authors brought out the worst in me. Nasty ignominious stuff and certainly not researching.

But the main problem, which dwarfed the date/age/lifestyle obsession, was my inability to stay awake very long in the library. The chairs were too comfortable, the air too charged with positive ions, the reading room too full of grumpy faux academic types leafing through back copies of Debrett's Peerage, the laptop room (another ghastly innovation at the LL) TOO FULL of clicking, humming laptops, and I, if none of the above had put me to sleep, too full of food to be able to stay awake for more than half an hour. At university, I had spent long hours sleeping in libraries and had been rewarded with a negligible degree as a result. In those days, sleep was the only form my revolt against "the system" could take.

But I also loved libraries. I loved the fact that each long-forgotten book could be a door into an unknown world. I loved the connections one could make, going from reference to reference, digging side shafts that joined up with each other. I loved the way books reached back into the past.

An empty library would be fine—no assistants in red T-shirts making a noise as they replaced books off the trolley, no readers clogging every table with their heavy books, no librarians ready with a direct-debit form to cover all outstanding fines—just me and the shelves, my metal-tipped shoes ringing and singing off the cast-iron floors of the stack rooms.

£D

BRIGITTE ARRANGED for me to meet Lord Howland, Herbrand Russell's great-great-grandson, in a very expensive fish restaurant. She intimated that only the best would do for Lord H. He was my age, tall, and with that curious complexion you sometimes encounter on very rich men. Their faces have a sort of 3-D effect, as if they are wearing makeup, except they aren't. It's as if wealth has provided some secret extra nutrient to their eyebrows and lips, making them stand out in comparison to the pale features of the underpaid, or the ghostly features of the flat broke.

I became fascinated by his 3-D face and by the way he handled Brigitte; not literally, of course, since her husband was also there, but in his disarming jocularity I detected both politeness and an engaging lack of care. The tiny London world of stress and tube trains and year-end bonuses did not affect him. When I suggested I visit, he said, "Why not come for a month? We had a sculptor down at Woburn for several weeks—he loved it."

Next to the phone call that changes your life, the invitation to stay as long as you like at a huge mansion is another key item of wish fulfillment. Unfortunately, I was not in an ideal situation to take advantage of such an offer, what with the sudden looming appearance of fatherhood. But I'd definitely stay for a while, maybe more than once.

Lord Howland said that he would recommend me to Maja Boyd, the world expert on Milu, who often spent time at Woburn.

Brigitte paid the bill, which was huge.

BUSINESS

THE STYLE of book we were aiming for usually featured men of science from the past who were either the first to do something or else solved some knotty scientific problem.

All I had to do was turn Père David and the Duke of Bedford into eccentric obsessives, reveal a bit of science in an interesting way, and somehow give the whole thing a global relevance, and we'd be in business, big business.

Back at my buzzing, humming, whining, crashing computer, things were more difficult.

DIRT

THERE WAS no "inside track" on Père David. No dirt, no weirdness. He was a good man, by all accounts, and "good" is hard to do on paper.

Herbrand Russell, the 11th Duke of Bedford, was slightly more promising. I could cast him as a crazy mixed-up duke—he'd saved a species, but he'd also introduced gray squirrels and muntjac deer into Britain. Muntjac deer were merely an interesting pest, but gray squirrels had driven the native red squirrels into endangered isolation on islands and in the north of England.

FORGETTING MILU

IN ANCIENT Chinese literature there is little written about Milu. In A.D. 300 it was recorded that a herd of fifteen hundred swept through the emperor's camp. Five hundred years later, there was a single reference indicating that the only such deer in existence were incarcerated in a forbidden game park. Sometimes the imperial family even forgot that Milu existed. As a child, the eighteenth-century Emperor Qian Long asked the eunuchs where he might find the animal that sported antlers like those displayed in the palace. He had to wait until he was emperor before the grand eunuch told him that Milu lived in his backyard, so to speak. Death sentences awaited anyone, bar the emperor, who attempted to catch one of these protected deer. There was no profit in even talking about them.

BLUE PETER

I NOW REMEMBERED an episode of the children's program *Blue Peter* I'd seen years before. Over a series of painted stills, one of the presenters—Peter Purvis, I think—had narrated the story of Père David. Père David, or Father David as they called him, had been the real focus of the story, and the Woburn part was not mentioned. Father David was a missionary who loved animals, a sort of modern Francis of Assisi. While China burned during some revolt or other, he sneaked into the Imperial Gardens and spirited away a herd of his beloved deer. He secretly shipped them to a zoo in France. Word then arrived that the remaining deer had all been slaughtered in China and that Father David had saved the species—and to this day they are still called Pere David's deer.

It almost goes without saying that *Blue Peter* was about a thousand times better in those days. There was no irony, no "cool," no pandering to the imagined attenuation in children's attention spans. This was before someone decided that all children were thick.

TOM

BACK THEN, in the early 1970s, my step-great-grandfather, Grandpa Tom, was nearly ninety. He must have been nineteen or twenty in 1900, when he fought against the Chinese in the Boxer Rebellion.

Grandpa Tom had a glass eye and a missing finger, the right index finger. Both these deformities were endlessly fascinating to a child of seven. I used to hide under the kitchen table just to be able to get a glimpse of his finger stump when he was sitting down. He never took his glass eye out and it was never referred to. Once, when he was laying the table for lunch, he put the pudding spoons next to the knives. "Not like that!" I piped up. "There's more than one way to lay a table," he replied, continuing in his own mysterious way.

Whenever he traveled, Grandpa Tom traveled light. Ex-soldier that he was, hated carrying anything, so whether he was going for a week or a month, he'd simply pop his razor into his top pocket and be off. If he needed to sleep, he'd sleep in an armchair.

Grandpa Tom had a wooden box in his caravan, and later, when he moved with my grandparents to a house in Stratford, it rested on the mantelpiece in his room. The box, which was an old-style portable desk, contained medals, old coins, an Argosy paperback, a German-issue Swiss Army knife, and a few photographs. One was of a street scene in Peking, taken just after the Boxer Rebellion. It showed a Boxer having his head chopped off. Behind him you could glimpse other heads in ominous pools of black blood. Grandpa Tom often passed this photo around at Christmas.

CHINESE MIRROR

I BEGAN TO notice in myself the same condition I'd observed in others who have to deal with China. It becomes impossible to be impartial. One swings between loving the Chinese and hating them. A kind of fake objectivity can be simulated by swinging back and forth as often as possible, but one is always taking a position. On a personal scale, to know that someone dislikes you has a similar effect—it is hard to be neutral toward them.

I realized I would have to go to China to see Milu for myself, returned to its native state in the former Imperial Park south of Peking. This travel-book side of the project would make the book exotic and more attractive to publishers, Brigitte said (and I agreed).

To make the proposal sizzle even more, I filled it with as many interesting facts as I could find.

My favorite fact was the discovery that the Chinese had a system of volumetric measures that worked by sound. The measures were like scoops made from brass, and each size had a precise tone when struck. In other words, they were like bells that could be used to scoop precious spices, and because a tone could be so accurately determined, they were very accurate measures. If a trader with musical inclinations wanted a certain weight of something, he just hummed the right note. I decided this promising lead should be followed up, so I embarked on a mammoth reading of Joseph Needham's *Science and Civilisation in China*. The gist of this huge work is to demonstrate how the Chinese thought of everything first. It makes dispiriting reading for confirmed believers in Western superiority.

Père David, it is true, by discovering Milu had saved it from early extinction. And in Woburn, Herbrand Russell had played his crucial part. But before that, the emperor who had placed Milu in captivity had been the first of Milu's many saviors. In 1150 B.C., Empress Tanki built a great marble House of Deer, one of the world's first zoos. Almost certainly Milu would have been among its captives. But this early zoo did not survive long. Neither did Emperor Wen Wang's Garden of Intelligence, a fifteen-hundred-acre zoo of around 1000 B.C. The unknown emperor who saved Milu had something different in mind. He incarcerated Milu in the Nan Haizi Deer Reserve for the selfish purpose of hunting. Through this simple self-interest he had saved the species for perhaps a thousand years, since all the evidence suggests that Milu had been extinct in the wild for a thousand years when Père David first caught sight of them in the Imperial Park.

SELLING YOURSELF

Y EARS AGO, just after I left university, I was an insurance salesman for a month. I'd had to pretend I cared more about insurance than I really did. But after a while, I really did start caring about insurance.

SOLD

S EVERAL PUBLISHERS had been hooked by Brigitte. I attended meetings where I did my routine. Offers were made. Just when it became necessary to decide which publisher to go with, I had the chance to go on a Ray Mears survival course. Ray Mears probably knows more about survival techniques than anyone else in Britain and I'd wanted to go on one of his courses for years. I borrowed a mobile phone and set off for the woods.

At night, in my leaf shelter, I made surreptitious calls to Brigitte. Mobile phones were not exactly banned, but Ray Mears ran a tight ship and I sought his approval. If he walked past I hoped he would just think the pressure of having to survive had made me start talking to myself. When I finished my calls I walked past other leaf shelters and heard the low murmur of others talking to themselves, until I realized that everyone had a mobile but was just too embarrassed to admit it.

We're on a survival course, learning how to make fire using a bow drill made of sycamore, and we're phoning home using microwave technology when we think no one is looking.

Before I went on the survival course I thought that everyone else who went on such courses would be weird, but they weren't. As a cross section of society the people on the course were actually very sane. The would be survivors were interested in many things, capable, fun to be with, serious when it was necessary to be serious. The only time I sensed a hint of madness was when we were all skinning rabbits, each survivor, including me, trying to impress the others with his willingness to get stuck in without being at all squeamish.

It was the day after I made fire using the bow drill that Brigitte made the deal. It wasn't quite as much as I'd hoped in my wildest dreams, but it was still a lot of money. Crouching in my leaking leaf shelter, I spoke with genuine gratitude to Klaudia at Auk Books, who had agreed to publish *Milu*, as the book was then titled. I called Brigitte and said how amazed I was that we had done the deal. "I'm not amazed," said Brigitte. "It's a good idea. Now all you have to do is write it."

KLAUDIA

K LAUDIA WITH a *K* was American, from New York. I'm sure she was born somewhere else, but all her references were to New York. She had big glasses with ironically tinted plastic blue frames that made me think of a butterfly having crash-landed on her nose. She was extremely polite and flattering but strangely assertive. If I said something she didn't like she'd just say, "I think that's a terrible idea."

Klaudia assembled a group of executives from Auk Books to say nice things to me in an office with a round coffee table. I say executives, but actually they were people who had followed very similar trajectories to myself until they were twenty-two or so. Then the divergence began. They drew salaries and had jobs where they decided budgets. I'd never done that. In fact, the last full-time job I'd had had been seven years earlier, driving a delivery van in London.

But in those intervening seven years I'd become wary of "suits," "salarymen," "straights," "stiffs." This wariness was partly due to the increasing confidence of the suits I met. When I was just a year or two out of university, the suits had lowly jobs and doubted whether they'd done the right thing. They were the ones eating bitter. But as the years went by, they got more and more interesting and well-paid jobs, whereas I just stayed the same.

I set aside my envy and hatred of suits in order to charm my way into the Auk Books fold.

I was glad that Klaudia was American, since Americans are my favorite and most hated people.

BLAG

K LAUDIA, A late-twenties editor at a prestigious publishing house, meets ROBERT, an early-thirties writer who has just been signed in an expensive Notting Hill restaurant. KLAUDIA has a terrible flulike cold, and ROBERT is keen to get as much value, i.e., free drinks and expensive dishes, out of the situation as he can. ROBERT is also somewhat nervous (Americans do that to him), and when he is nervous he drinks and smokes to excess. KLAUDIA gamely drinks wine with ROBERT and politely swallows a few whiskeys to help "cure" her cold.

ROBERT later hears that KLAUDIA has had a complete relapse and spent a week in bed recovering, though, in keeping with her tough persona, she never mentions this to him.

BLOCKAGES

THREE MONTHS went by. I was supposed to be busy continuing my research into deer. The signing money took longer than I expected to come through, and my willpower and single-mindedness seemed to be fading. In previous bouts of research I'd been much more ruthless, but this time any excuse pulled me off course. When I had only written about myself it had been easy to keep on track. History was different. Every time I tried to surge forward I just ended up going sideways. It was as if I'd hit this invisible wall and I was just circling it, circling endlessly. For days I wandered deeper and deeper into the forgotten byways of Anglo-Chinese history, discovering Morrison of *The Times*—the most famous correspondent of his day, a former doctor, who couldn't manage a word of Chinese—and his one-time assistant, the mysterious Edmund Backhouse, a disgraced scholar/intelligence agent who masterminded a fraudulent diary of the dowager empress. It was Backhouse who promulgated rumors that foreign dignitaries were forced to kiss the naked pudenda of the empress before matters of state could be discussed.

I read for days, often getting up late and then reading until four or five in the morning, forcing myself back to sleep with a dry mouth and a febrile buzzing imagination.

I was scheduled to meet Klaudia to discuss my progress with *Milu*. When I tried to assemble my "progress," it all spread out sideways and didn't amount to much. It was just my record of circling that wall, a wall I couldn't see over, didn't know what was beyond, didn't even really know for sure was there. It was like a sci-fi force field repelling me each time I approached. Of course, this kind of talk is not publishing talk. In publishing terms all I'd managed to do was assemble bizarre facts about people who had very little to do with deer.

The day before our powwow I stayed up late, drinking and thinking. Nothing.

The next day I had one of those hangovers that are manageable as long as you do not try to think too much. It's as if the brain is a volcanic crater and you're just allowed up to the edge, far enough to see a ring of glow and no more. It's as if thinking can only take place in the outer millimeter right next to the confining skull.

Skirting around the edge of the crater as I traveled to the Auk offices, I decided that *Milu* had to be "about" something. The obvious, possibly tabloid, über-theme was extinction. OK, the concern for the deer would be an example of our fear of extinction, which has mushroomed in this century. Mushroomed because of the—yes—atomic bomb. I was ready for the meeting.

KLAUDIA sits in her tiny office behind a desk piled high with manuscripts. ROBERT sits, well wrapped up in scarves and sweaters, on a plastic chair in front of her. ROBERT is already on his second coffee.

ROBERT: You see, I asked myself, Why do we care? Why do we care so much about some bird or some insect that's about to be wiped out forever? Why? Because we're frightened of our own extinction, as a race. And for the first time since Stone Age times the existence of the human race is under threat. The A-bomb. The H-bomb. We don't give a toss about insects being wiped out—we're worried about ourselves.

KLAUDIA: Absolutely. These are all important themes. But tell me, how do you visualize the cover?

ROBERT: I see an H-bomb exploding. I know it's a clichéd image, but if we could get a rare photo of, say, a Chinese H-bomb, that would be really good.

(A beat as the true enormity of the divide between them sinks in.)

KLAUDIA: Do you know what I see? I see Milu on the cover. Milu is the hero of the book. Milu has to be the star.

ROBERT: You're right. Absolutely right. Milu is the star. We can't pretend he isn't.

KLAUDIA: But Milu isn't Bambi.

ROBERT: No. Absolutely not. Not Bambi.

KLAUDIA: But we need to grab people straight away. So I see you following a hunting expedition in Texas on one of those exotic game ranches you told me about. That's how the book opens. You watch how some wealthy hunter kills an endangered species.

ROBERT: Fantastic. We love Milu immediately because we've, er, killed him.

KLAUDIA: Not you. You just have to tag along and observe. Maybe you could cover it for a magazine. One of those men's magazines you write for.

ROBERT: It's brilliant. Start with the deer being killed. Milu is the hero. Père David. Eleventh Duke. Deer returned to China. Fantastic. I think we're all done. Let's get some lunch.

KLAUDIA: (*looking puzzled*) Yes, OK, fine.

They go to a medium-expensive restaurant for lunch.

KLAUDIA talks glowingly about a famous Auk Books author who always pays for the wine even if the publisher is buying lunch.

Despite hearing this, ROBERT again feels constrained to stretch Auk Books' largesse to the full. He angers the crater of his hangover, which erupts into a throbbing headache somewhere on the train journey home to South London.

EGYPT

AFTER A *few days in Egypt I started fasting, though my wife said I didn't have to, despite it being Ramadan. Technically we were on a journey, and fasting is not required of the sick, the pregnant, or those making a journey. But I wanted to fit in, and I felt that the challenge of fasting would be good for me. Bizarrely I thought it would help the book, give me more inspiration.*

Before this, the longest I had been without food was twenty-four hours. But even then I had smoked and drunk water. An Islamic fast is a total ban on anything going into the mouth from dawn (about 4:30 A.M.) until dusk. No food, no cigarettes, and no water. Because it was winter, it wasn't so hard. Dusk, which was when the fast could be broken, came at 5 P.M. Surely I could stick it out until then?

My mother-in-law had set aside a room for me to work in. On the first day I sat down and wrote, "Once upon a time." It felt good, as if I were tapping some source of unlimited story power. I felt hungry but I soldiered on. That first day I did several thousand words, inventing a bizarre mythology for the appearance of Milu on this planet. In a nutshell, it was because the gods were bored with regular animals so they invented a whole host of freakish animals such as Milu, duck-billed platypuses, flying snakes, and dwarf kangaroos. At that time, defeated by the task of writing a straight "objective" book, I had decided to turn the whole thing into a fairy story.

That first day I had two baths, a nap, and a walk along the Nile. It wasn't a great time to take a walk because I was there just as the Iftar traffic madness started. Iftar is when the day's fast is broken. Everyone has a feast of sorts. Beggars and the poor are invited into street tents paid for by rich men and are fed handsomely. The rest of the population tries to get home or to a friend or relative's house. Because everyone is starving, the meal has to start on the dot of five. So the preceding hour is absolute mayhem. It took me almost fifteen minutes just to cross the road alongside the Nile.

This was the first time I'd noticed how the car population of Cairo had rocketed over the past five years. Also, the cars were newer—far fewer beaten-up old American cars and fifties Mercs. Egyptians were getting richer.

The first few days of the fast were tough. I had a headache, and when I sat down to write it was as if there were a clanging empty space in my head with no power to produce words. My main thoughts were directed to the area from my sternum downward. During Iftar, I gobbled far too much food in too short a time. On day two I thought I might have a hernia, or some other serious internal rupture, my stomach was so uncomfortably tight. It almost felt as if I'd strained an internal muscle, or a tendon holding my insides together.

BASQUE COUNTRY

SUDDENLY I'M in the Basque country, winging along a two-lane road that I remember from fifteen years before as one lane; but never mind, the sun is shining, it's late May, and I've managed, at least for a while, to escape sitting in a library or staring at a blank computer screen. I am with my old friend Justin. Justin and I were at university together. When we're together we talk a lot about people we both knew at that time. Justin is very good at doing impersonations, and he can still impersonate people we made fun of fifteen years ago. When he does it first, I can then copy him. So our knowledge of the past gets reinflated. He remembers things I'd forgotten and vice versa. We were going to be together for at least a week, Justin and I, so our joint knowledge of the past should increase considerably.

Justin does a job that pays him a lot of money. He needs the money to buy the things to live the life he wants. But he also thinks he works too hard and is wasting his life and that the things he buys are just distractions to keep him working too hard to buy the things to live the life he thinks he wants to live when he isn't thinking the opposite.

He knows I vaguely disapprove: perhaps of his wealth, perhaps of his superior social standing, perhaps of the fact that he works too hard. It's never fully explicated, since the purpose of the past, and our talk about it, is to divert attention away from having to talk about anything uncomfortable. That can be a bad thing, but not always.

We were on our way to the birthplace of Père David. Justin was driving; I could tell he preferred it that way.

I knew from past experience that whoever drives the car first, if it's a rental, becomes the surrogate owner of the car during the holiday. They call the shots. But even knowing this, I let him take the wheel. The sun was shining and it was a lovely day.

Whenever a car tailgated him (which was often, since we weren't driving very fast), he slowed down even more in the hope of making the car overtake. It was a vain hope, since drivers in this part of France prefer tailgating to overtaking. They just slow down too. This agitated Justin. "I bet your father does this too," I said, and Justin just grinned sheepishly. A few minutes later he made a jokey comment and grinned impishly. It's easy to travel with someone who has both sheepish and impish grins in his repertoire.

Père David was born in the Basque country in 1826, in a tiny village called Espelette. As a boy he'd run up and down the Pyrenees and this had given him a hardy constitution. Years before, I'd walked the Pyrenees and I knew the terrain was steep and often unrelenting. After two months of walking there my calves had doubled in size. I thought a lot about Père David's legs, how they must have been muscly with strong, thick-kneecapped knees. Whenever I thought of Père David he sort of flashed his legs at me in my mind, lifting up his ecclesiastical robes to reveal a fine tanned pair of hiker's calves.

Père David was no writer. His diaries are opaque and workaday, his major work, *Les Oiseaux de la Chine*, hardly self-revelatory. After his Basque upbringing, he attended the Grand Seminaire de Bayonne for two years. In 1848 he entered the order of Saint Vincent de Paul. Followers of the order, which had been set up in the seventeenth century, were known as Lazarists. Like the Jesuits, they practiced a new kind of monasticism, more interested in educating the poor than living in monasteries. They were called Lazarists because their headquarters was in the Saint Lazare district of Paris.

Père David wrote constantly to his superiors, asking them if he could travel abroad. They sensed his restlessness and tested him by sending him to cool his heels and teach science for ten years in a Lazarist college in Savona, on the Italian Riviera. While there, he made a natural history collection that attracted the favorable attention of the Natural History Museum in Paris. He also inspired several students to go onto greater things, including d'Albertis, who attained fame as the ethnographer of Melanesia.

Two years after arriving at Savona, Père David wrote:

I am getting on in years and am almost twenty-seven and want to go to the Celestial Empire, Mongolia, and other similar places as soon as possible. . . . Thank God my health is excellent and my always robust constitution will enable me to undergo the life, fatigues, and privations of a missionary. My desire to go to the missions is motivated in part by a desire to do penance, but also by the belief that since childhood God has called me to this.

After eight years of such importuning, the bishops eventually gave in and let Père David go to China. He arrived in 1861 and stayed, on this first trip, until 1870. It was in 1865 that he discovered Milu.

Even reading between the lines, I began to realize that there was no skeleton in Père David's closet. He wasn't a dirty monk who studied botany in between studying boys' bottoms; he was a clean-living, observant, honorable, and kindly man. That was why there were no biographies about him. I wasn't about to give up yet, though. I thought about those bulging calves, built by running up and down mountains.

Actually, the country around Espelette is about as mountainous as parts of north Kent, or the Cotswolds—hilly, yes, but not mountainous, not really.

ESPIRITU SANTO

INTO THE thick glass killing jar twelve-year-old Armand David rammed withered leaves of laurel. These were high in prussic acid, the bitter-almond juice that became cyanide gas on evaporating from the cracked leaves. Absorbed through an insect's carapace, it would first stun and then kill.

David took care to roll the jar in a long piece of cloth, which he then tied around his waist. His calico tunic shirt had belonged to an uncle and was spotted on an elbow with delicate blue stitches as small as pinheads.

David ran up the hill to where he had seen the insect. On the chipped and polished bark of an old oak was a six-inch-long praying mantis, bright green, with sprung muscular forelegs locked together as if in prayer. It moved its head surprisingly out of motionlessness, dead alien eyes in its tiny green mask. A diviner, the Greeks thought, and, by the doctrine of signatures, believed to have divinatory powers. Prie-Dieu, they called it in the village. David already knew its real name, *Mantis religiosa*; all real names were in Latin.

But how to catch the damn thing? Bring the jar down quickly, and a leg could be broken, or the insect might fly off. It might leap and spit at him; the cunning boy in the village said the spit from Prie-Dieu could cause blindness.

David had caught cicadas before, snatched them out of the air, and this was no different. It was just about steeling himself and not thinking too much, moving now while he had the chance and not missing it like the other time.

He moved his hand forward tentatively, realized this was no good, withdrew, and watched the insect some more. Then he reached out quickly, almost without thinking, and the mantid body was between finger and thumb. He could feel the dull rustle as it tried to escape. The boy stared at it up close, seemingly fixated, before dropping it into the jar. Then he turned the jar over onto the dry earth.

How long does such an insect take to die? He stared through the bubbly blue-tinged glass, but it was hard to see and the mantis was hidden by laurel leaves.

He stared further, out across the land toward the sea. David scratched his legs. Now he really was a scientist.

He took in the view without sentiment, interested only in calculating the distance. Today he hadn't faltered and he hadn't needed a second chance. Not like that trout he'd "tickled" in the Latsa River—twice he'd failed to snatch it! The third time he'd grabbed ahead of its habitual escape route, and the slippery thing flew hard into his hand. He'd killed it reluctantly on the bank using a giant blue pebble to beat its head into stillness.

The mantis must be dying now. David dragged his shirttail along the stony soil and under the entrance to the jar. Upending the jar and shaking down the leaves, he put the wooden lid in place before pulling out the cloth. David secured the killing jar with string, then sniffed his shirttail for the sweet, headachy aroma of bitter almonds.

BIRTHPLACE

WE FOUND without difficulty the birthplace of Père Armand David. It is now a butcher's shop. We asked the butcher if he knew anything about the history of the house, anything more than the plaque on the wall.

"I'm not from round here," he said, smiling a big red butcher's smile. He explained in detail that he came from a town four miles away.

"Could we look inside?"

He couldn't say, he was renting the apartment to someone else.

A head appeared at the window above, a middle-aged, harassed-looking woman with her hair unraveling. "There's no point," she said. "It's completely changed since Père David's day."

'How does she know it's completely different unless she knows at least a little about what it was like before?" I asked. The butcher agreed, but she had shut the sash window by then.

We visited the mayor, who was planning a commemorative garden to honor Père David. As well as mayor, he was also president of the Friends of Père David. We had to winkle this out of his secretary because I think he wanted the Friends of Père David to appear as large and as impressive an organization as possible. The mayor, an athletic-looking fifty-year-old man, had even looked into the possibility of obtaining a Pere David deer for the garden. But he said that the foodstuff and vet bills would have been too expensive. (Actually, they live on grass and, if they fall ill, usually die before a vet can save them. Perhaps he meant the high cost of the deer—at least four thousand dollars each.) A giant panda was out of the question too. "There's no bamboo in the Pays Basque," said the mayor. "Nothing for a panda to feed on." The mayor was going to make do with a garden of exotic plants that had been discovered by Père David.

We gave the mayor a donation and wished him well with the garden, which was still under construction.

KILLING AND EATING

PÈRE DAVID favored the most basic forms of travel—either walking or riding mules and donkeys. He always took with him a faithful servant, Sambdatchiemda, a former Buddhist monk from Mongolia who had converted to Christianity, and sometimes Sambdatchiemda's brother, who wasn't a Christian. But that was the extent of his entourage. He wasn't a big-shot explorer with a hundred coolies hefting barrels of butter and cigars on their backs. Most of the time, Père David lived on vegetables. He was frequently set upon and robbed like the character in the Good Samaritan story, except, in his case, no Samaritans turned up. Once a group of bandits announced they were going to kill him and eat his liver. Père David brandished his gun while Sambdatchiemda led the mules to safety. Night was falling and in the confusion both men escaped with their livers.

It was rough going all the way, and I'm sure it was the scientific nobility of the project that inspired Père David. He ate vegetables not for the usual vegetarian reasons—in Peking he had enjoyed his meat and fowl. But he felt that if he killed animals for food on an expedition, it would change the status of the animals he killed for science. Perhaps it would make his effort more ordinary, reduce it to a kind of hunting trip, like shooting ducks in the Camargue, nothing to write home about. Sambdatchiemda sometimes begged him to shoot a pheasant or two for the pot. With a ruthlessness I didn't really admire, Père David always refused.

FLOWERING

SOMETIMES THE rats come first and sometimes the flowering of the bamboo. In cycles of almost fifty years, the bamboo of all Asia flowers but once and for a season and then is quiescent for another half century or so. The rodents stampeding through every clump of bamboo from Yunan province to the Naga Hills are there to eat the seeds that spill from the flowering plants. How do the rats know when to run? How do the bamboos know when to flower, all of them at once across half the surface of the planet?

Père David had established his usual efficient herbarium operation under the creaking canopy of giant bamboos in the country

of Muping. He had taken it upon himself to instruct Sambdatchiemda's brother in the useful art of something—in this case,
pressing and drying flowers.

Sunlight flickered through the green leaves, a steady breeze
inducing two hollow bamboos to knock together with the carrying tonk of a wooden bell. The ground was dry, and it was easy to
set up the tabletop on two wooden seed boxes.

Unlike Sambdatchiemda, his brother was quick to learn. First
he took the specimen *Davidii involucrata,* which some of the locals
called "dove tree." A more common name was "ghost tree." This
came from its appearance when in bloom. The white flowers
resembled the pieces of paper hung in trees to appease the ghosts
of ancestors.

The young Mongolian removed the hard-packed red mud from
the wooden stem with the porcupine-quill brush favored by his
master. He then pointed to the most shapely specimen of leaf and
translucent white flower before snipping it off with the one-piece
clippers like ancient sheep shears. David nodded each time as the
young man explained how he would next proceed. The priest's
deep-set eyes were diverted for a second by a sound from the specimen box on the leaf-littered ground. A large gray rat appeared,
nuzzling out of the box. Sambdatchiemda's brother kicked at the
rat, an instant arc of foot and leg that set the creature screeching
against a bamboo trunk. It was an alarm call to the rest, and ten
more rats skittered down vertical bamboos and over the rotting
trunks on the ground.

But a few rats were not worth even a comment from the priest.
Not after the plagues they had seen. Since *Involucrata* was not
fleshy like a *Brassica* or *Euphorbia,* there was no need for the copper

boiling vessel, which sat handily on iron feet above a quick fire of twigs. When the water was boiling, any fleshy plant was blanched like a lobster to kill its growth. David had learned as a boy that fleshy plants will grow for a month in a flower press unless cauterized first in boiling liquid.

To preserve the white of the flowers, his young assistant placed the plant section in the top part of David's mahogany smoking box. He then lit a sulfur candle in the lower section and allowed the harsh smoke to play up through the drilled holes and over the petals. The altered paleness of the plant would revert to its original color and remain fixed for years after this treatment.

Handmade drying paper, made by monks for filling the nostrils of the dead, was found by David to be excellent for keeping the specimens apart.

The wind was getting up again, knocking together the elegant curved bamboos. It was strange that flowers and rats should go together.

CLOCKS

WHEN PÈRE David arrived in Peking in 1861, he was expected to teach science in the Lazarist missionary school. There were only two other teachers: one taught math and the second taught horology. These were the subjects the Chinese were interested in. Having a third of your curriculum devoted to clockmaking was particularly interesting, and a throwback to the old Chinese obsession with striking clocks.

It struck me that the Western interest in time was functional, whereas the Chinese interest was more mysterious.

Striking clocks arose in the West so that monks could rise and pray at the same time each day. More and more uses were found for clocks and they improved year by year.

But in China, the knowledge of how to build striking clocks was actually lost from the thirteenth to the sixteenth century.

Why were the Chinese so much thicker than the Europeans?

I must apologize here to more balanced readers, but if you had stomached thirteen hundred pages of Needham on the utter superiority of the Chinese you'd want to throw a few spanners into his argument.

I mean, if you're so brilliant at inventing things, how could you forget how to make something as relatively simple as a striking clock? It's not a computer, which depends on all sorts of subsidiary technologies, or a Mars Bar, which depends on remembering taste, etc. Imagine trying to reconstruct a Mars Bar from a drawing in a sixteenth-century monkish manuscript.

How could a culture be so careless as to forget a vital technology such as clockmaking? Or, more importantly, how could a culture go technologically backward?

This seems to me to be the big question. Chinese culture didn't disintegrate. Lots of other inventions were remembered. It was just that one of the more esoteric forms of technology was lost: striking clocks.

Even a few steps backward, technologically speaking, seem impossible here in the West. Though we are quite used to seeing other things disappear, or get worse. We blame these disappearances on technological progress.

Losing skills, for example—skills connected with trades that have been superseded. No one can cut the hubs of cartwheels using just a hand ax now. In fact, when I told a skilled carpenter that this was how it used to be done (the source was a nineteenth-century memoir), he assured me that it was impossible, that pole lathes had always been used. But the memoir had explained this, that the very best wheelwrights had insisted on showing their skill by carving entirely by eye using a small ax.

In other words, we have lost skills in the West that we can't even imagine now. But since we value *things,* we still know how to make them (even if the ways of making things have sometimes changed). I can't think of one thing we've forgotten how to make in the West.

What else have we lost? The possibility of certain experiences: to go one's whole life without seeing more than two or three visual images, hear only live unamplified music, travel no faster than a galloping horse.

Without the Jesuit "invasion" of China, the Chinese might never have learned how to make clocks strike again. The knowledge could have been lost forever, extinct.

In the grand scheme of things, losing the ability to make striking clocks is trivial. There are a million more important things than this, even though it is symbolic of a careless attitude to technology. An attitude that would be regarded now as very backward.

In the West, the sheer bulk of techno-information, whether on computer or in books, shows how important we think science and technology are. No one is ever going to be allowed to forget how to make anything. Though the very bulk of techno-info that stops us forgetting how to make things actually causes problems of its own. This huge weight of knowledge serves to squeeze us poor humans. Its sheer bulk diminishes us.

If you are connected to an institution that controls part of this knowledge—a government department, a university, a high-tech company—you feel empowered by your connection; high on science. But this empowerment obscures something. It masks, through its socially approved bulk, our real need for truth. And anyway, in our own quiet real lives, away from our brightly lit desks, this techno-information is no use at all; it does not lead us toward a better understanding of life, or ourselves.

Of course, there are many *material* benefits provided by science and technology, but what I'm talking about here are the psychological disbenefits. By promising hope of solving "life's problems" and not delivering, technology, if you take it as seriously as it wants to be taken, cheats us of life, offering superficial diversions in place of sincerely sought answers. It is a kind of extinction too.

RELATIVES

WE LEFT Espelette village and its prosperous red-roofed houses—all that EU money to local farmers, we concluded. Back through the green hillocks to Bayonne to meet Père David's oldest living relative, Mme. David. Actually she was only a relative by marriage, her late husband, Charles, having been Père David's great-nephew. Mme. David was ninety, but very spry, sitting under a trellis of vines in the cool courtyard behind her house. Her maid brought us coffee, and Mme. David told us that the secret of a long life was to be "old in the head but young at heart." She smiled and took a sip of aniseed water; she'd already had her coffee that day, she explained.

Mme. David had the most perfect place for sitting outside. It was like one side of a cloister and abutted the house, cool and open to breezes and hung with vines that occluded the archways into the garden courtyard area below.

Mme. David had been born in Chile, though she was of Basque origin. Charles had met and married her out there while working as a surgeon in a tannery town. Other descendants of Père David had moved to America and Bolivia. Mme. David felt pity for "pauvre Pinochet," who was at that time being hounded for murders committed during his regime. She and her husband had left Chile during the time of Allende. "A terrible time," she said, but left it at that. Never worrying about anything was another secret of long life, she said.

She showed us books owned by Père David that had remained in the family, including letters and an article with notes. His handwriting was neat, thin and compressed, written with a hair nib, and barely legible.

Holding these old books that he must have held, I felt, or imagined, a connection to the old priest. Some of the books were gifts to his nephew, Mme. David's father-in-law. The book *Voyage en Mongolie* (1875) was inscribed, "A Monsieur Joseph David, souvenir de son oncle, A.D."

Père David set up no great institutions, wrote no great works, but he cared deeply for his two nephews, in a homely, nonshowy way.

Before we left, Mme. David told us that another secret of long life was caring for other people. "If you have no one to care for, pff, you are useless." She showed us the place where her husband had hidden wounded members of the Resistance during the war.

MILU

How he found Milu is the best part of the story. Père David was marooned in Peking, again cooling his heels. His superiors had decided he'd been on enough trips into the wilderness for the time being. His robust health had broken down and he had been ordered to recuperate. Reluctantly he agreed and set about organizing his Chinese science students to help him start a cabinet of curiosities from the environs of Peking.

One student was reportedly an obdurate fellow. He could see no point in the priest's insistence that students bring in dead animals, insects, and birds. Père David tried persuasion: "The study of spiders alone proved that Italy had touched the continent of Africa in ancient times. Such is the utility of Natural History collecting." When reason did not work, he threatened the student with punishment if he didn't produce something interesting. Spluttering with rage, the student informed the priest he would bring him Su Bu Xiang. The other students went silent. The naughty fellow realized he'd gone too far. No one was even supposed to know of the existence of the famed beast with four characteristics that did not match.

Père David questioned the student quietly, after the lesson. All that he could discover was that the animal was kept inside the for-

bidden deer reserve of Nan Haizi, south of Peking, and that soldiers who guarded the park called the animal Milu.

The next day, Père David rode by sedan chair the ten miles
from Peking to the forbidden park. He walked several miles each
way around the wall, which was eighteen feet high and over seventy miles around. The chance of even catching a glimpse of
Milu was zero.

Months later, the same recalcitrant student supposedly provided Père David with the clue he needed. The area around Nan
Haizi had been badly flooded, and part of the wall of the Imperial Park had collapsed. The only thing was, the student didn't
know which part.

Père David set out to walk the entire seventy-two-mile circum-
ference without a second thought. Walking, we know, was something he was good at. The priest believed in the purifying effect of
long-distance walking. It was simple and hard work. The diges-
tion was stimulated, the muscles toned, while the mind could
wander in meditation or prayer. It echoed the purposiveness of
early pilgrims. Man as walker is our most ancient inbuilt image of
higher purpose, of truth-seeking.

He set out, and after several miles was rewarded by the sight of
a huge gaping hole in the wall of the Nan Haizi reserve. Through
the hole, which was blocked with a flimsy line of wicker hurdles,
he was able to see deer grazing. And he could hear something
strange. The sound of their feet clicking, something only reindeer
do. But these were not reindeer.

Père David was longsighted and quick-sighted. He noticed
that the antlers on these deer seemed to face backward and that

their tails were long like those of mules or horses. Then a guard appeared with a giant billhooked spear, and the gentle priest made his way quickly home.

Père David had taught himself written Chinese and he now referred to texts lodged in the ancient Hanlin Library, in a building next to the foreign legation in Peking. He found a librarian who knew his way through the great encyclopedia of Yung Lo Ta Tien, which ran to over eleven thousand original volumes. Here he found mention of Su Bu Xiang, a creature supposedly created by the gods as an afterthought, using parts from other beasts, as if the creativity of the deities had run flat and they were reduced to mixing and matching various odds and ends. They were so pleased with these experiments that they retained a white Su Bu Xiang to pull one of the chariots of the ancient gods. Along with the tail of a donkey, the head of a deer, and the neck of a camel, Su Bu Xiang had the hooves of a cow, except they clicked. Père David had formally identified Milu.

In the Chinese method of classification, Su Bu Xiang belonged with other creatures that failed to match the morphological ideal of deer, beetle, hawk, or trout. Milu languished along with other oddities of nature: lampreys, leaf bugs, flying foxes, and mouse deer. But just as the gods take away, so they have to give, in order to preserve the celestial balance of the world. Milu and its freakish cousins were believed to be imbued with special powers. The fact that they were of mixed inheritance meant a fourfold increase in protection against death, a poetic prefigurement of the notion of genetic diversity as a guard against disease. Unfortunately, Milu had been hunted to extinction in the wild because of these reputedly health-bestowing powers. To live off the meat of Su Bu Xiang meant increasing one's life expectancy fourfold. No wonder only the emperor was allowed to hunt them.

An ordinary priest would have let the story end here, but Père David was now committed in his own mind to securing a specimen. Only with a specimen could a scientific discovery be made. And in the obsessive world of Père David, scientific progress was equated with religious devotion. Work was prayer.

The problems at this stage were seemingly immense. The deer were forbidden to all but the emperor, and the guards had a free hand to kill anyone trying to poach one of their animals.

Père David wrapped several pieces of silver and a note in Chinese inside a piece of soft leather. He returned to the place where the wall was being repaired and, having caught the eye of a guard, threw the bundle high over the wall. The note indicated that he would return a week later to the spot and pay another quantity of silver for a Su Bu Xiang carcass.

He arrived at dusk at the hole in the wall, which was half repaired by now. Two hours later, the same leather bundle came hurtling back to him. Inside was another note: Send money first and we will send deer.

Père David scribbled a hasty reply and, having thrown it back, walked away. He pointed out he'd paid half the money already and that they were beholden to trust him, not the other way round. He would return a week later for the deer.

Sure enough, on his next visit, after a short wait, the remains of a recently butchered female came flying down from the ramparts wrapped in bamboo matting. Père David sent the rest of the money back over the wall.

After embalming, the creature was sent to France by diplomatic bag, contents undisclosed, courtesy of the French ambassador.

In Paris the professors were ecstatic. They demanded a living specimen.

DARWIN

EXTINCTION WAS a controversial subject in Père David's day. The unexplored world was shrinking, and it was becoming increasingly implausible that dinosaur bones belonged to a species that still existed in some remote region—the old, and more attractive, explanation for fossils. Georges Cuvier, excavating in the Paris Basin, broke with the past and announced his belief in the widespread extinction of dinosaurs. Charles Lyell, Darwin's contemporary, was not convinced: he clung to the ancient belief in the immutability of life on earth. Darwin, of course, provided the hammer blow to such thinking.

It was just a question of time, therefore, before the possibility of the extinction of the human species became a widespread idea. And when it did, the fact of the A-bomb and biowarfare simply made it more concrete, more tangible, the fear already in us. Making extinction a necessary part of life added a shadowy bleakness to the scientifically informed worldview. The theoretical necessity of extinction leaves the world a little colder.

EGYPT II

I AM GETTING *more used to the fast. It doesn't do to overeat at night, certainly not the sweets that everyone guzzles. Nor is it worth getting up at 4:30 A.M. for a predawn snack. Better to shorten the day by lying in bed. At first I was swamped by all kinds of paranoid and irrelevant thoughts. Now they have melted away. My head is clear. When you don't eat or drink for hours, your thoughts become razor sharp, echoing off the metal balloon of your skull. I realized that most of my thinking until now had been made muzzy with partly digested food and drink.*

The worst part is the way time just stretches away in front of you. Nothing to break it up. It's like being on a long car journey inside your head.

MAJOR II

As soon as I got back from the Pyrenees, I started looking for new excuses to leave my desk. As a sort of research-related project, I attended a meeting of the League against (modernizing) the London Library. It was there, on 31 July 1999, that I met the Major.

He was a vigorous, elderly man, much impressed that I had been in search of the longest snake in the world (for a previous book). Fortunately, I spoke very little about Milu, and the Major seemed perfectly at ease doing most of the talking. It's what he seemed used to. At first I thought he was some kind of bizarre salesman. He wore a silver shellsuit and a chunky gold ID bracelet on his wrist. His teeth were yellow and strong, and he grinned like a friendly predator. He was silver-haired, almost bald, with a nicotine-stained handlebar mustache. Eventually he invited me to his club. A place I could hardly imagine existed except as a sick joke: the Extinction Club, where members vied to exterminate every last one of any given endangered species.

SURVIVAL

EXTINCTION. THE very word is uninviting. Dead volcanoes, dodos, and dinosaurs. The past known only through fossils. That which could not survive. And in this century, to survive is to be good. To survive is to be a genetic player. To survive is to obey, according to the religious dogma of the age, the highest imperative of the species. "I'm a survivor," someone says. And we know exactly what they mean. What if someone announced, "I'm not a survivor?"

Survival. I love the word. *The Survival Handbook* by Anthony Greenbank was my sacred text from eleven to fourteen. The book was banned briefly at twelve when I was caught climbing down a loose drainpipe, following the suggested method of escaping a burning building, except our house wasn't on fire and my mother was watching. It was reading this book that made me, years later, want to take a Ray Mears survival course.

SURVIVOR

UNTIL THE mid-twentieth century, the word *survivor* meant an individual who had survived a specific life-threatening situation. One was always a survivor *of* something. There was not, as there is now, an acceptable usage of the word as a general description in which no specific event has been survived. Despite everyday life being more hazardous in the past, simply surviving life did not earn one the title *survivor* as it may now.

The change in usage is mirrored in the change in the way we use the word *victim*. Victims and survivors are connected through this modern usage. A victim who overcomes the disabling effects of his situation becomes a survivor. It is very tempting to categorize everyone as either a victim or a survivor. Though there is an innate pessimism in this way of classifying ourselves and others, it seems appropriate given the low expectations we all have of actually changing anything on this planet.

And we have not just low expectations of change, but also very strongly felt concerns about the safety of all of life on earth. Governments armed with powerful weapons of mass destruction may kill, by design or accident, millions of innocent civilians. Biocorporations busy splicing genes could accidentally release a deadly microorganism.

Suddenly we are no longer safe. And by this I mean that, even if I wanted to, there is no longer anyplace left to hide.

The experiences of World War II seriously weakened the vocabulary of morality and ethics and introduced a new value system more suited to the perceived powerlessness of those who suffered in the war. Uniquely for a war, it was convincingly demonstrated that many noncombatants suffered more than combatants. Few soldiers would have exchanged their experiences for those of a citizen of the Warsaw ghetto, Hiroshima, or Dresden. No authority or government came out of the war unscathed. The crimes were perpetrated by governments against powerless individuals. Being unarmed and unable to fight back, the victims of government bombing and persecution became martyrs. But it was a new kind of martyrdom. People were martyred just for being alive, for being in the wrong place, for being human.

Illness and misfortune have always struck. A plague such as the Black Death must have caused an almost paralyzing fear. But from the beginning, some people survived the plague. Accidental immunity to a disease provides a way of escape, a place to hide.

But when a government decides to drop its full atomic load, we perceive, perhaps wrongly, that the possibility of survival, even in a lead-lined bunker, is zero. Life after an atomic holocaust is unimaginable, except in movies and comics. *Holocaust*, in both its Nazi and atomic-warfare usages, has come to signify an event that is unthinkable in some way. It's a warning word, warning us not to attempt to be pragmatic in this zone of the unthinkable.

In the late 1970s, British local government officials, when told that only they, and not their families, would have a place in the command bunker, formally decided that if the bomb was dropped they would hurry home and ignore any orders to descend underground.

As long as the bomb doesn't drop, the nerve gas descend, the GM supervirus infect, we are entitled to call ourselves survivors.

The archetypal survivor is the inmate of a concentration camp. He is someone who has no control over his life in any normal sense and yet he somehow survives. He may trade his cigarettes for bread, or his skill at making musical instruments for cigarettes. Or he may be someone graced by incredible luck—in a fireproof building when firebombs are dropping, or in hospital when fellow inmates are selected to be killed.

The survivor "gets by," "keeps his nose clean," doesn't attempt to fight the system. Instead, he uses knowledge of the system to his advantage. But he cannot hope to confront or change the system; in his heart he knows that his is the life of a cockroach, dodging the heavy aimed boot of a house-owner.

The survivor cannot really afford to enjoy life. Enjoyment suggests a surplus of opportunity the survivor just doesn't have. In order to survive he has to wear blinkers. So in his survival lurks a kind of death, a giving up of what is vital and human, the joy and connectedness of life ground down by the gray demands of the day-to-day.

And very many survivors of the Holocaust, when prompted, reply: "The best did not survive."

SURVIVALIST

A SOCIETY OF only victims and survivors is a stable society. Think of a prison in which no one wanted to escape or even take over the warden's office. Such a prison could run forever. If we can talk of society having its own mechanisms for self-perpetuation, then the survivor–victim dichotomy would be one such, very handy, mechanism.

The survivor is useful to society. He provides a role model for a kind of dogged helplessness. The survivor accepts his powerlessness in the face of the power of the government. He hopes simply to survive, that's all.

The popularity of survival training is due, in part, to its promise of increasing the control one has over one's own life. Control is returned to the individual without the need for complicated machines or large amounts of money. He can become self-reliant rather than dependent. To make fire with a bow drill of dry wood is to be liberated from the technology of matches and lighters and the money to buy these things. The liberation may only be symbolic, but it is a symbol one can carry around in one's heart, a psychological fall-back position for when the going gets tough.

Likewise the study of self-defense.

These attempts to master a simplified environment empower people who feel overwhelmed by modern life and its strident demands for dependency.

So, unlike the survivor, the survivalist is an enemy of present-day society.

The survivalist is lampooned for wanting to make things hard for himself, for trying to turn the clock back on all our amazing timesaving technology. He is regarded as odd for wanting to be self-reliant. Odd because he doesn't like cars and TV and shopping. In the future, though, perhaps the desire for things will be seen as odd in comparison with the desire for human qualities.

DETERMINATION

THE MAJOR and I—he was now in a jacket and tie but still with the clanking ID bracelet on his thick wrist—sat in leather wingbacked armchairs and waited for the results of his latest extinction. With his graying eight-inch handlebar mustache, the Major was known to be a stickler for punctuality. He implied that the committee of the Extinction Club respected this. The mustache, like the Major, was a wily old survivor. During the appalling tedium of one summer in the Lahore barracks, the Major (then a subaltern) had embarked on a mustache-growing competition with the now late General Sir John "Bull" MacIver. By the time of the first monsoon, the mustaches were set to be measured by an agreed-upon group of trusted fellow officers. It was generally accepted that Bull would win. His handsome dark nine-incher bristled farther and finer than the flaming red handlebars of the Major.

But Bull, by his boasting, had put himself at a disadvantage. He had underestimated the mean single-mindedness of the young Major, who came from no rich and distinguished family, had no famous forebears, had not even attended a very good school. The young Major was a self-made Englishman, and he had never lost at anything.

The night before the monsoon, when everyone came down with headaches and the wind whistled in the neem trees, the young Major lay awake, his cruel blue eyes pinpricks of light in the darkness. At three o'clock, he leaped from his bed, the moon casting a sliver of light over his pillow. Dressed in a singlet and army shorts, he climbed like a cat out of his window and up onto the roof of the barracks. Along the roof, hanging down to check the sleeping form of MacIver behind the extensive tent of a mosquito net. Down, soft and quick onto the dusty floor, along to the net, out with the kukri. The gleaming crescent of razor steel cut the net. There lay the sleeping Bull—baronet, good sport, generous to women, wealthy, intelligent, a mess-room wit, universally liked, and soon to be sporting a one-handled mustache.

The cut was quick and delicate and reminded the young Major of an almost forgotten youth helping his father to slit the crops of chickens choking on stalks of grass.

To leave the hair or not? Better to take it. Disposed of in the endless cow-dung fire of the nightwatchman.

At six o'clock in the morning, a howl of anguish rang the entire length of the barracks.

EXTINCTION

LET US divide up extinction into more manageable pieces.
First, there are the great extinctions caused by climatic shifts.
It's simply too hot or too cold for something to survive. This kind
of extinction we can understand, since the change of climate
attacks food supplies and all aspects of habitat at the same time.

Then there are the extinctions caused by hunting: the dodo
and the solitaire supposedly come into this category.

Then come the other kinds of extinction, which are altogether
more mysterious. Some species are too rigidly specialized. Their
lack of adaptability to even small changes, changes so minute
that they do not register as such to us, causes them to die out.

As humans we rightly value the ability to adapt to new surroundings. Those who don't, we cheerfully label *dinosaurs*. Com-
panies that can't adapt deserve to go bust.

And don't we feel, deep down, that those species that have
become extinct somehow "deserved it" too, that their very inability to survive was a moral black mark against them? By a curious
alogic, not surviving means you didn't deserve to survive in the
first place.

Push this only a little further and aren't we uncovering a morality no different from that of the crudest eugenics, the well-
intentioned Swede rounding up and neutering "mental defectives"?

CLUBLAND

THE PRINCIPLES behind the Extinction Club were simple. Members paid handsomely for the privilege of exterminating an entire species, wiping it off the face of planet Earth, leaving behind no zoo specimens and no pets—total eradication. There is a saying of the Prophet Mohammed that it is not wrong to kill animals, they are put there for our benefit, but it is forbidden to kill a species. The Major, despite his disdain for women (they were all either "cats" or "old cats"), clergymen, and the concept of original sin, was not a Muslim, but he did sympathize with that religion. On this point, however, he and the prophet parted company: the Major had no qualms about killing off an entire species. He had so far dispatched several types of tree vole, a South American beetle found in only one square mile of forest near Belem (he paid for the Brazilian Airforce to napalm the area, reducing each tree to a smoking stump), a blind fish found only in underground wadis of Saudi Arabia, and his latest triumph: poisoning an entire lake in New Zealand with cyanide for the sole purpose of eradicating a species of clawless crayfish.

By modern standards, the Major was a very evil man, though he had killed no fellow human (in the war he was involved in training and planning) and had committed no crime until this unexpected burst of lawlessness in his late seventies.

As a member of the League against (modernizing) the London Library, the Major despised the casual clothes and red T-shirts of the staff—reminiscent of Romanian fascists, he said. He hated computers and had a particular dislike of being quizzed by female librarians. If one of them remarked on some overdue item when he was taking a book out, he would ignore her, remaining cold and unspeaking, until the most senior male member of staff came to her bewildered rescue.

When the Major realized I wasn't a pinko liberal (or was too intimidated by him to reveal my true colors), he launched into a monologue that outlined his main beliefs. We were sitting in the Extinction Club's plush headquarters, waiting for the crayfish lab results, which were being Fed-Exed from New Zealand.

The Major was smoking hard black Brazilian cheroots, his tiny wicked eyes glinting with forceful malicious humor.

"Only five percent ever counted in this country, and their numbers were decimated in the Somme and Passchendaele. Elimination of the officer class, you could call it. England has been going downhill ever since."

"What about Churchill?"

"That weeping egotist! We might have been better off under the lunatic Hess."

The eyes glinted. Interruptions, I quickly gathered, were not required.

"Having killed off the genetic stock that counted, it was only natural that we let go of the empire. Indeed, once I realized the tragically low caliber of men being sent out to rule India, I was in favor of disbanding the empire as soon as was practical. Of course, the Indians and the Africans have made a terrible mess of things, but we just didn't have the moral force anymore.

"You ask why I should take such pleasure in killing. In fact, I don't. I have my own reasons why I engage in this kind of work, and they are none of your, nor anyone else's business. I consider myself, in a global, cultural sense, to be extinct already. My views exist only in the addled brains of delinquents and madmen. Whereas before I stood with kings and heroes. We are entering dark times. My own peculiar racialism and prejudice against the fairer sex will be seen as mild buffoonery compared to the harsh world that is coming. The planet grows madder and madder, and I shall be glad to be soon gone.

"My work, my lasting legacy, will be made known after I die. Perhaps people I have taken into my trust will speak about me. If they do not, I have taken measures to ensure that word will get out. People will be baffled and appalled by my actions. Indeed I estimate that I will remain largely misunderstood until the twenty-second century."

He stubbed his cigar out with a workmanlike flourish. The committee chairman was making his long way toward us across the plush green carpeting of the club. I noticed the bronze "feet" that held the soft carpet in place. The Major continued: "When the smoke has cleared, your great-grandchildren may understand."

"Can you tell me?"

He tapped the side of his nose, on which grew an unusually large bulbous mole. "Work it out for yourself," he smirked.

"Major, Major," bleated the committee chairman, "I am pleased to announce *Lophophorus ibuysil* no longer exists." The Major raised his eyebrows and nodded at me in a meaningful way.

PSEUDONYM

I T WAS all getting a little mad. I'd wanted to help reform a library, and here I was being drawn into a global eco-terrorist conspiracy—but on the wrong side. The Major's ideas made me sick. Even his view of Darwin was perverted. He believed that the logical outcome of Darwin was not diversity but a single species. The idea was that chance mutation would simply endlessly improve one species as it moved from environment to environment, wiping out other species as it went. All Darwin predicted, said the Major, were extinctions. He said the only thing Darwin had been correct about was multinational business. The growing similarity of every high street from Uxminster to Ulan Bator was single-species proliferation at its most obvious. Whatever I thought about such bizarre ideas, I knew I mustn't let on about Milu. Using my research, he could conceivably orchestrate their successful elimination, there being fewer than two thousand in existence and all locations well documented.

I suggested to Brigitte that I write the book using a pseudonym, something like Alan Potts or Benjamin Dale, a name that couldn't be connected to me. She was unhappy about the suggestion. She pointed out reasonably that the publishers would want to publish *me*, not just my writing skills, whatever they might amount to. *Me* included the interviews I'd done, the reviews I'd garnered, the TV program I'd been in. *Me* was practically becoming a brand, whereas Alan Potts was nothing, as anonymous as baked beans in a labelless tin.

"It's so hard to establish any kind of presence in the market-place," said Brigitte, when I suggested that a book about deer might confuse readers of my earlier book about martial arts. "Any publicity is welcome, and what we already have we should use."

I left her intimidating office feeling lightheaded. Being Alan Potts could have freed me up. I could have had fun. I could have forgotten about my "style," the readers who said they were look-ing forward to my next book, the people who had already mocked my ideas. I could have forgotten about the Major. For the first time I felt the burden of being me.

HAIR

THE BURDEN of being me. As long as I had to be me, I was concerned about the things that increasingly concerned me. My nostalgia for the past, for example, which kept getting in the way, shouting at me that this was the story, the real story: how everything old and interesting and valuable was just disappearing.

When I was eight, at the height of the fashion for long hair, I'd given myself a short back and sides with the kitchen scissors. My grandmother had laughed when she found out, but Grandpa Tom said nothing. I knew that he knew that the haircut was a sign of allegiance, with him and with the past.

Grandpa Tom's own hair was cut in a back room at the pub by a retired barber. Grandpa Tom and his farmer friends would have their hair cut there on a Thursday. The only barber's in town was now unisex, and even knowledge of how to give a real short back and sides was disappearing. Who would cut Grandpa Tom's hair when the retired barber died?

FREAKS

THERE IS no word for *definition* in ancient Chinese. Instead, Hsun Tzu's term *Chih ming*, "management of names," was used. It reflected an ambivalence about nailing down the essence of a thing with words. Aristotle thought essences were easily nailed down. The Chinese sages were not so sure.

Milu's classical name, Su Bu Xiang, or the animal with four characteristics that do not match, is somewhat vague, but an excellent description once you have seen the animal.

This poetic method of categorization meant that Milu might share a theoretical category with an opossum or a duck-billed platypus—animals that combined defining traits from different groups.

So Milu sounds like an engaging freak, like an entry in a Borges short story.

The ungainliness of Milu reminded me of the dodo and the solitaire. Of course, Milu didn't lack the ability to run, but the meat was known to be exceedingly good, just as dodos were known to be very tasty.

Milu liked to splash around in marshy places, even in winter. Perhaps this meant they could be easily targeted.

Another unsupported theory: I am inclined to believe that the freakishness of the beast, just as with the odd-looking dodo and solitaire, prompted some deep-seated viciousness to surface in humans who encountered it. There is something of the victim about these creatures. They look like animals you can bully. Baby chicks and puppies bring out our parenting instincts. But freaks bring out our unlovely instinct to keep the gene pool clean, untainted, unweakened. Perhaps at some deep primitive level there is a program in our brains to eradicate abnormality, oddness, eccentricity, wherever we meet it.

The bully victimizes those who look different, but they have to look different in the right way. Individuals who look stronger or more beautiful than average look different in an acceptable way. They are there to strengthen the species. And they look more at home than the rest. Freaks always look as if they don't quite belong, as if they have strayed from where they are most at home, their manor, patch, turf, 'hood, demesne.

A bird that can't fly has forsaken its natural home; a flightless bird is a refugee, just waiting to be picked on. And Milu—a deer that might be a cow, or a mule, or even a weird kind of camel, with its big, trusting eyes—where would that be at home?

Perhaps nowhere except in a sanctuary for such similar beasts, a kind of refuge like the forbidden park behind its high impenetrable wall. It seems to me that once we bullying, freak-killing, eccentric-hating humans arrived, Milu's only hope was to be in a protected place.

Did the emperor who decided to save Milu in this way (the anonymous first savior of the animal) understand that he was, in more than one sense, going against nature?

SNAIL

A T 5:30 P.M. on I January 1996, the last surviving snail of the species *Partula turgida* from French Polynesia died. This must be the most precise documentation of an extinction ever carried out. We can only speculate on the exact circumstances surrounding the last dodo or the last mammoth, but with the tiny (thumbnail-sized) snail from the Pacific, we know exactly, because the snail was part of a conservation program set up in 1987 in the London Zoo.

The aim of the project was to protect *Partula* from extinction. It was the most spectacularly unsuccessful conservation project in history.

Native *Partula* snails had been suffering hugely because of the introduction of *Euglandina rosea,* a vicious killer snail that was not a Pacific native. *Euglandina* had been introduced to kill off an epidemic of escaped African land snails. These too had been imported, as a food item, presumably to satisfy a taste for snails on the part of the colonizing French. If the islands had been colonized by the snail-hating English, the train of events that led with plodding tragedy to the final extinction would never have happened.

The story interested and amused the Major so much that I began to wonder if he had been hovering near the London Zoo that January day. In between bursts of peculiarly impersonal guffaws, he explained why this was a perfect extinction.

(i) It was caused by the French.

(ii) In earlier stages it was a random sequence of events that brought the snail to the brink of demise. How could anyone foresee that wanting a delicacy for dinner would result in the complete disappearance of a species?

(iii) If the only fully documented extinction was such a random event, how could we hope to prevent other extinctions in the future?

"By locking up people like you," I remarked, knowing this would amuse the Major. He guffawed again, then grew serious.

"My little excursions are beside the point. The eggheads at the London Zoo really believe they know how to conserve the animal life of this planet. But they cannot even save a snail. Other forces keep living creatures alive. Other forces! Perhaps you might not ask this question if I told you that the greatest threat to the animal kingdom comes not from pesticides or nuclear waste but from the way we think. A species dies because we can no longer think about it in the right way! We kill it with our thoughts. After that, twenty drums of cyanide dumped in a beautiful lake is a mere afterthought."

I almost became angry. Except I knew that that was what the Major wanted. He was watching me with his beady, alert, compassionless eyes. Waiting for a sign of weakness on my part.

EGYPT III

FTER A *week I have read all the books I have brought with me to Egypt. I need books. It becomes an obsession. I am only writing three hours a day—even if I get up at nine, that still leaves five hours until I can break the fast. I have never known such an insatiable desire for reading. Perhaps it is because I am fasting, nature's way of distracting me from my groaning stomach. But more than the distraction, my perpetual hunger focuses my mind, makes it clearer than usual—how right, I marvel, the universal religious requirement to fast.*

I was already familiar with most of the new bookshops in Cairo: the American University shop; the French bookshop run by a smart Coptic woman who insisted on speaking French even if you spoke her first language, Arabic, to her; Madboulis for translations; the German bookshop for books in English about Egypt; and failing all those, the sometimes surprising selections in hotel bookstalls. My wife took me to all these places, but it only satisfied my need for books for a few days at most.

Then she took me to the most overpriced secondhand bookshop I have ever been to anywhere in the world, including Tokyo, Nepal, New York (cheap), and London. The shop specialized in books about Egypt and the Middle East. The prices were so high as to make you stare intently at the neat pencil numbers inside the flyleaf—no way, you're thinking, no one would dare ask that much.

The only "cheap" things in the shop were prints of old maps and old postcards, at three Egyptian pounds each, and modern guidebooks. These items sold well. I never saw anyone buy a secondhand book. Then I deduced the logic. The books were not meant to be sold. They were too valuable for that. They were the bait to get people into the shop. Once there, the extremely high prices of the books would make the slightly high prices of the prints look cheap. People would buy these, leaving behind the books. It had probably taken years to assemble such a fine and complete collection of Egyptiana. It might take years to replace it—so why sell? Use it to sell something cheap and replaceable like the prints or the thousands of tatty postcards.

The old books were functioning like the Pyramids: there to attract tourists (well, that's their function now) who could then be persuaded to buy carpets, papyrus maps of ancient Egypt, brass incense-holders, miniature stuffed camels with real leather harnesses, and conical wooden ballpoint pens turned from cedar wood.

At first the high prices in the secondhand bookshop sickened me. But when I realized it was a scam to sell cheap prints, I didn't mind anymore. In a way, I admired their business acumen, the thickset knitting woman who sat next to the wooden-drawered till, an eye on everything, and her articulate son talking American tourists through a hinged folder of prints.

But I still needed my fix. From a hotel bookshop I reluctantly bought a Lonely Planet guide to Cairo. I'd read it quickly, I thought, then ditch it. For an LP guide this one was OK, though the tone of the author was pure back-packer—politically correct with a disabling dose of relativism balanced against a fun-seeking, anti-Islamic chauvinism. This guide announced categorically, on page 174, that there were no secondhand bookshops in Cairo.

FAMOUS PHOTOS

THE ADVANCE money had finally come through. Using this newfound wealth, my wife and I were able to move to Oxford. My parents lived nearby and said they would help when my wife had the baby. Leaving London was also a good way of putting distance between the Major and me. I'd been a student at Oxford, and the Bodleian Library, while less exclusive than the LL, had far more books. I had no friends in town, but that changed when I met the Novelist.

Years before, I had read his first novel and liked it. I found it darkly humorous, though in the end the dark did overwhelm the humor, but I didn't tell him that until much later. Coincidentally we both lived in Oxford and both had Klaudia as our editor. Klaudia gave my book about Japan to the Novelist, who said he found it funny. We agreed to meet for a pint in a pub where there was no music.

That first meeting was great. The Novelist told me all sorts of interesting stories about his travels and painted a great and lasting portrait of a place in the Welsh borders where he had spent two summers in a disused barn and the local undertaker had also been the publican. If Graham Greene veers uncontrollably toward whiskey priests, then the leitmotif character for the Novelist would have to be publican undertakers and the kind of humor they entail.

The Novelist's great hobby was photography. Later I was able to admire many of his photos, but at that first meeting, or maybe the second, he told me something very interesting, almost in passing. He said that a survey had been done to find the three most famous photos in the world, and not just among Americans and Europeans but Chinese, Africans, Peruvians, and Melanesians as well. In doing the survey, people had been dispatched into jungles, deserts, and mountain strongholds armed with an ever-shortening shortlist of photos. From these the most recognized pictures were selected.

They were (a) the picture of the atomic mushroom cloud, (b) the picture of Earth taken from outer space showing it to be blue and wisped with cloud—the picture that proved conclusively that the Earth was round, (c) . . . but the Novelist couldn't remember the third most famous photograph. I made several suggestions. None was right. Whenever conversation slackened I kept returning to this game of thinking of the famous third photo. The Novelist joined in at first, but after a while I could tell he found it irritating.

I should explain about the Novelist's name. Though I had read his book, I had actually forgotten his name. Somehow we managed to meet without me remembering the name Klaudia had told me. Then it became too embarrassing to ask his name, and when I discovered his name after asking someone who had also read one of his books, I wasn't sure how to spell it (it's a strange spelling of a familiar word), and all this time I was thinking of him simply as the Novelist, as if he were a character in a Tarkovsky film. And actually, when I met him, I did think he looked a bit Russian, a heavyset blond engineer from the Ukraine specializing in very heavy machinery, perhaps, or a deep-sea trawler captain from frozen Murmansk. The Novelist.

BREAKTHROUGH

SURVIVING AS a novelist is a difficult business. It's hard enough to get people to remember your name, let alone buy your books. If a bookshop sells your book and doesn't reorder, then the slim spine advertising your wares has disappeared. And as a writer, you begin to disappear.

Klaudia at Auk Books had very high hopes for the Novelist's latest novel. It was his fifth novel, but the first for seven years, and it was being touted as a "breakthrough" book.

The breakthrough book is a mysterious concept. Everyone knows a book when it has broken through, but no one is quite sure how to make that happen. The breakthrough happens when the writer ceases to be just a name on a book with the same status as a name on a bank-account application form and becomes something different, more intimate, almost part of the family.

A breakthrough is referred to, by people who have met him, by his first name or his last name—depending on which sounds coolest or most intimate. Dean R. Koontz is probably referred to "in-house" as Dean rather than Koontz.

Sometimes the public have never heard of a writer who has broken through. This can be embarrassing—at book signings, for example. But the public knowing your name is merely a sign of celebrity. The real judges of breaking through are the trade and the press. Sometimes, bizarrely, the only knowledge they have of such an author is the fact that he has broken through. Generally this means the interviews with the author will cease to question his existence, his right to write, as it were, and concentrate instead on the pleasurable experiences the interviewer is having interviewing the author. Of course, there is a whole rank of other journos just waiting in the wings to tear into the breakthrough author, but often their evil attentions just help him.

So the breakthrough has two effects. First, the outside world gives you permission to exist. Second, and more importantly, your books stay on the shelf in the bookshop. They get reordered. The book is given an extra chance to live.

Klaudia hinted that the Novelist was about to break through. Somehow I expected it, even without being told. Maybe it was some mysterious vibe the Novelist was giving off. Outwardly, I noticed only one sign that things were changing, and that was the brand-new deluxe laptop he had allowed himself to buy.

DIARY

I was getting used to living in Oxford again. I had my routine of reading and writing and visiting Blackwell's bookshop and having occasional drinks with the Novelist. I had taken to working in the garden in a shed with windows. It was pleasant looking up from my screen at the trees, but there were few birds, and no sparrows.

I should have applied for a Bodleian Library card to carry on my research, but I told myself I'd do that very soon. Even though I had left Oxford twelve years ago, a lot of people still looked vaguely familiar. But the only people I identified positively were freaks and outsiders. Maybe they were more noticeable. Or maybe freaks and outsiders change less with time. Or maybe Oxford exerts a strange magnetic pull on such people.

I saw the College Weirdo, or CW, in a supermarket. He was far thinner than I remembered him, and the slight resemblance to a bird had come right to the fore, a beady-eyed heron or wading bird with a neck that can bend backward to gulp down fish.

The CW didn't recognize me, because I only spoke to him twice when I was at college. Both times it was to ask for the salt. Back then he had been thirty-five when most students were twenty. He had been studying for some obscurely defined postgraduate degree, but had stopped halfway. But he still came into college every day, to eat alone in the great dining hall and later to have coffee, usually again alone, in the Junior Common Room. It was as if he were saving up his voice for Friday night, when he would command the Union debating chamber with his stentorian gibes/comments/interjections/musings, which always wiped the floor with the speaker and brought the house down laughing at his Oxford cleverness, his wonderful timing. To hear him in the chamber was to hear him alive, existing in the gay crucible of hard-ened glass that is public life. He never stumbled and he never hesi-tated—qualities in a debating adversary that are greatly unnerving.

Then they discovered his diary. Or rather, in an act of incredi-ble folly, he left it lying in the Junior Common Room after he had finished his coffee. The diary made its way through several hands on its way to the dean, a blunt, modern, officious man, friendly but intolerant, one suspected, of weirdos. And the diary, which contained at length the CW's sexual ramblings over a Welsh girl of, it had to be admitted, considerable beauty, left the dean with little choice but to take action. Word was already out. The girl was wor-ried, didn't like the way he looked at her, now she remembered. The diary was rumored to be well written, but of extraordinary filth. The CW was banned from college. He continued for a short while to attend the Union, but his prospects were less than they had been. Years needed to pass for people to forget. He gave up public speaking forever.

Twelve years on and he is birdlike and unbeaten in the super-market. He looks fresher and healthier than he did, but dreadfully thin. He's nearly fifty now, closer to death than to the halcyon days of university.

The College Genius is also kicking around. Also thin. His first essay took fifty-five minutes to read out, which left only five minutes for discussion, but since he'd said everything, there was nothing left to discuss, so the tutorial finished early.

His downfall came when he inexplicably didn't get a first-class degree. From this blow he never recovered. Still kicking around, same part of town as the Weirdo, the posh end, a few miles from the colleges. I saw him in the off-license buying fizzy white wine. He looked frail, older than his years.

PULPED

WHAT I admired most about the Novelist was not his amazing flat on an island in the River Thames, nor the collection of excellent photos he had taken on his travels, which adorned said flat, nor even the fact that he had set foot on every single continent and visited over a hundred sovereign territories. What I admired most about him was his staying power. He'd published four novels, the last seven years ago. All were out of print, despite having won prizes and special awards and having garnered goodly praise in the serious reviews. "You know the most chilling words you can ever hear?" the Novelist used to joke. "You're pulped." Once he had rung the publisher's warehouse to see how many copies of his novel they still had in stock. "Sorry, mate," said the warehouseman. "We pulped you this morning. No copies left now."

You're pulped. The book has not just gone gracefully out of print. It has been exterminated by an avaricious publisher eager for warehouse shelf-space. Imagine how big a warehouse is. Imagine ever running short of space in a warehouse. Imagine how much space a thousand paperbacks take up. Nothing. Or next to nothing. Less than a cubic meter. You're pulped. Mate.

But the Novelist had fought back. In the seven years since the horrible pulping incident, he had written and abandoned several drafts of the novel that was now being touted as "the breakthrough." In between, he had been on a screenwriting course in a vain attempt to learn the more lucrative art of writing for TV and the cinema. "Basically, I was crap," he said, a broad challenging smile on his face. The Novelist didn't want anyone to think he had grandiose notions about himself. Praise, if it came, would ring a silent inner bell that the Novelist kept hidden behind his trawler-captain exterior, and no one would know that the critics were right except his secret inner self. That he had a high opinion of himself I have no doubt. All writers do, though the areas of pride can vary, and English writers are very canny at keeping a low profile.

The Novelist had kept on writing, returned again to the novel, gone to a deserted barn in Wales with the manuscript, written another draft, and then another. And now it was going to be his breakthrough novel, of that we were all convinced. And I assume, though I can't be sure of this, that the advance matched the publisher's expectations. He had a new G3 laptop, after all.

BOOK DEATH

How does a book die? How does it become extinct? When nobody reads it anymore? When nobody buys it anymore? When libraries won't stock it? When nobody remembers having read it?

A book is a piece of the writer's life. It is all those hours he sat alone talking to himself using a pen or a word processor, trying to both satisfy his conscience that he was writing some semblance of sense and keep his word count up for the day. A writer talks more honestly and less stupidly when he writes, or tries to. He's a better person, or trying to be. A book is a record, and like a record, a CD or an LP, it contains enough to summon up life for us. Just add water in the form of attention to the words, and life comes to you from out of the fingers of the writer, from his heart and his brain down onto the paper and then back through your eyes to your heart and brain. A book is an act of sharing some of your individuality with others; books are keeping something alive.

"You're pulped, mate," stops all that.

EGYPT IV

I AM WRITING *longhand and in notebooks with paper that is just too thin for an ink pen. Over time, this is disturbing. I want to think my writing is high quality, not leaking through cheap paper. Of course, when you start worrying a lot about the externals of writing it means the writing itself is lacking: prison memoirs written on toilet paper are the counterexample that is supposed to make you realize just how lucky you are. This neglects the very real need to keep up momentum through a convincing show of behavior. Morale can fluctuate; if there is a solid routine and ample physical evidence of progress (sheets of paper, words written and counted), then it is easier to power through the difficult times when everything seems hopeless and pointless.*

When I am not griping about my paper quality I am looking for excuses to go out to get more books to read.

My father-in-law takes a morning nap sitting in a chair on the roof of the building with his head wrapped in a towel to protect himself from the sun. The roof has been turned into a terrace with lots of plant pots and a trellis that partially shades out the sun. There are extremely realistic plastic vine leaves and grapes weaving over the trellis. When he finishes his nap I take over the terrace for my writing.

A further trellis that runs along the top of the wall around the terrace causes one to look up rather than out. Though it is December, the sky is always blue, and in the sun it is warm enough to wear just a shirt.

But even on this great terrace I think more about reading than writing.

HANLIN

THE HANLIN Academy, the famed "Forest of Pencils," contained the hive of examination cells where scholars from all over China were locked for nine days and nights while writing an "eight-legged essay." They slept and ate in the tiny five-foot by three-foot cells with meager bowls of cold rice pushed under the wooden gates each evening by suspicious invigilators intent on unmasking fraud.

They were right to be suspicious—in the quarter next to the Tsungli Yamen there were seamstresses capable of such minute embroidery that a whole book could be reduced to a tapestry of quotations tailored into the armpit of a gown.

The first exams had tested a wide range of subjects, from philosophy to horticulture. But by the late Ming they had become formalized into the rigorous literary form of interpreting the Confucian classics, the *pa gu wen*, or eight-legged essay. For six hundred years, mastery of this strange prose-poetry form was necessary for advancement as a mandarin. There is no Western equivalent of such a form. The nearest might be Kant's antimonies, where two opposing arguments are developed in columns side by side. But in the eight-legged essay, the columns answer and contrast with each other in tonality as well as content, like "a team of paired hoses."

READING ROOM

I REMEMBERED THAT smell—dry as dust, a hint of vinyl padded seats, the sweetness of floor polish, and dead books in rows, waiting to be exhumed. My reading ticket had been easy to obtain, once I had overcome my lingering qualms about going back to the place where I spent so much time not working so many years ago.

The Philosophy reading room in the Bodleian Library had hardly changed in twelve years. There were the same ever-so-comfy wraparound padded seats with arms that had sent me so unfailingly to sleep. The only noticeable change was the ugly rank of computer terminals near the book-ordering desk. The computers hummed and spread their mess of wires down the back of the table and across the floor. A few students were using them, but most were sitting at the tables—each with its own light—with a pile of books and paper in front of them. The students even seemed to be dressed the way I remembered students in my day dressing. Maybe they were a little less scruffy now, but I couldn't be sure. I revisited several old bookshelves, found a book by Collingwood, which was one of the few set texts I remembered reading with pleasure, stared aggressively at the computers, and left.

In a few years, nearly every book in the library will be on the Net. There will be no need to visit the library and fall asleep anymore, and that has to be a good development. Students can spend all their time in their rooms, which is what they like doing best anyway. The only reason to visit the library will be to look at unpublished manuscripts, the design and typography of old books, and to get a nostalgic buzz.

Of course, some books won't get onto the Net. Books published abroad by obscure publishers, or books the Bodleian committee have mislaid, or don't like for some reason.

Francis Bacon warned in the sixteenth century that many ancient scientific works were being ignored by the new printers. Since there were no monks working as scribes anymore, these books would die. Evidence from maps—which were still required to be copied by hand—suggests that exactly this did happen. A few old maps survived, but the books that supported the knowledge they contained died. Why? Because in the fifteenth and sixteenth century, people weren't interested in science. They wanted books of religion and entertainment and belles lettres. It was rather like the switch from LPs to CDs—the CDs in existence now are those that are in fashion now. No one is busy making CD versions of those LPs you find with chewed corners in the chuck-out box in a charity shop.

One sign that knowledge is at risk is how much effort we make to preserve what we already have. Ignore the efforts to find more knowledge—after all, we're not even sure it *is* knowledge until we've had it for a few years. And we're doing quite badly on the preservation of what we have. The British Museum employs seventy conservators. If the museum stopped acquiring books, it would still take those seventy conservators a hundred years to repair all the books that need repairing. In a hundred years, many books will simply crumble into dust. In fact, many will never be preserved, because the number of new books acquired each year is rising.

In some American libraries they have taken to ripping the books apart and scanning material in or recording it on microfilm and then simply burning what remains of the original text. The fires have already begun.

Every advance in information technology involves choosing what you want to preserve and what you want to ditch. Scanning rare books onto microfilm is a costly business. The library won't let you do it yourself—they decide first which books should be scanned and which should just rot away in the basement.

Against that eventuality, people should start hoarding the kinds of books committees of rational people will decide against scanning into a database.

BOOK DEATH II

I CASUALLY MENTIONED above about the books that get mislaid by library staff. But until it happens to you, with a book you really need, then it doesn't really make much impact. I mean, why should you care? It's just theory. But when it happens, the whole fragile edifice of the library becomes apparent.

I was in the Oriental reading room, using that as a base for ordering books from the colossal stacks of the Bodleian. It's a copyright library, so they should have every book ever published in Britain plus a pretty substantial amount from abroad. They have warehouses out in the countryside just groaning with books; sometimes they have to send someone out in a van to pick up your book from there. And beneath the whole of Oxford are vaults full of books, with an underground railway like something out of James Bond running from building to building deep under the tarmac.

The book I ordered was a diary of the Boxer Rebellion by Jessie Ransome called *The Story of the Siege Hospital in Peking.* The book was on the CD catalog of books published before 1920; it was on the computer, so it must be there.

I waited several hours and then went back for my book. The news wasn't good. They couldn't find it. The librarian had been herself to have a look, but there was no sign. No one had made any note of this, and because the system is computerized and since no one really knows how it works, there is no way of record-ing the loss, like scribbling a note on a file card, or even taking the file card out as an aide-mémoire for a later search.

That book, published in 1901, is now, within the hallowed con-fines of the Bodleian, certifiably dead. There is probably one in the British Museum, so it isn't desperate, but what is strange, or seems so to me, is that the book is registered as existing. If there was a fire in the Bod, then they would assume that the book had been burned, when in fact it had long been missing—lost or stolen, who can tell?

Historians are now of the opinion that both the great fire of the Hanlin Library and the fire of the library in Alexandria were actually rather convenient, since most of the books had in fact already been stolen or had simply rotted away. The fire merely drew a neat line under the whole miserable decline of the place.

This is how knowledge really dies, slowly, bit by bit, hardly noticed.

KEY TEXTS

THE JESSIE RANSOME fiasco reminded me of a central tenet of student life—the concept of the key text. The tutor would hand out a reading list with a hundred book titles to choose from. Only one would be the key text. The game was to find it and rewrite the crucial sections in order to score an alpha grade for the weekly essay. If the key text was not obvious, then the last recourse was to ask students in the year above. To write an essay without knowing the key text was a surefire way to a delta. This early programming was now apparent. Deep down, I believed that every subject had a key text.

The key text about Milu would start at the beginning, outlining the fossil record of Milu's ancestors (three-pronged old-world deer), move to sites where Milu remains have been found (Honshu in Japan as well as all over mainland China), proceed at length through the relevant ancient Chinese texts, contain a blow-by-blow account of mating, feeding, and territory-marking rituals (males splash their urine by swinging their penises from side to

side with a slight upward flick at the end of each lateral movement). Such a book would be based on the lifetime experiences of
a Milu watcher like Maja Boyd, the world's expert on Milu (who
had not yet responded to my attempts to get in touch).

I had been looking for such a book since the beginning, but
sadly even the vast resources of the Bodleian Library could not
supply me with it. Recovering from this blow, I redirected my
search to discover key texts of lesser magnitude and greater spe-
cialization. The Jessie Ransome memoir, based on her siege diary,
was supposed to be such a minor key text.

After reading a key text I'd have to feel I'd not only been there
but that I would know the significance of any fact I subsequently
came across in that field. Not knowing the significance of a fact is
the most worrying thing, if you're trying to get to the bottom of
a subject.

On one level the key text is just another word for a good crib. But
for me it means more than that. There is a certain feel, almost an
atmosphere given off, when you pick up a book in which the
author knows what he is talking about and is able to communicate
the important parts of his subject. Such a book is a key text. There
will be an absence of jargon in a key text, since no one who really
loves their subject can bear to see it shrouded in jargon. Unfortunately, the demands of modern science often mean jargon is
inescapable. For this reason many key texts were written in the past,
before scientific hegemony was achieved. People looked at things
just as hard in the past, and in areas where looking is important—
for example, in wildlife and nature observation—old books are
often superior to the impersonal compilations now produced.

X Marks the Spot

LEARNING HOW to get better at spotting a key text is not easy. It requires hours of dedicated browsing in libraries or bookshops, both new and secondhand. You can't learn this skill on the Internet. It certainly isn't taught in school, because most teachers don't have the skill themselves. And at university it may be hinted at, but all too often, as I have mentioned, it is simply for use as a crib. The significance of the key text is far more than that, and the ability to spot them is akin to having the art collector's "eye."

Which isn't to say one can't learn. Spending hours in bookshops and libraries gives one an overview of many subjects. It acquaints you with many books, and gradually, just as a wine taster develops a nose, the bookhead develops the ability to know how good a book is just by picking it up and flipping through a few pages. I'm not talking about fiction here; rather I'm talking about books that want to communicate information and know-how about a subject.

And strangely, when you know about the key-text concept, key text come looking for you, turning up (sometimes) at your fingertips just when you've expressed an interest in a subject. There are all sorts of rational explanations for this, but I find none of them convincing.

RESUSCITATION

I WAS STARTING to accumulate quite a library of my own. I used the excuse of writing about Milu to spend a lot of money on books about China, deer, and conservation. I could claim it back against tax, I told my wife. Actually, like most readers, I love buying books, especially in quantity. In a few years I can quite see myself going to auctions and bidding for boxes full of books I haven't even looked at, random selections of books, on the off chance of there being a gem buried in all the garbage. I could have a complex of sheds in my back garden full of these unopened crates of books. When things got dull I could just go out back and root around, looking for some lost masterpiece.

I was hoping that the key text (whether on Boxers, deer, or conservation) would turn up in a secondhand bookshop if it wasn't in the library. Oxford only has two or three half-decent secondhand bookshops, which is pathetic for a town of its pretensions. I visited these a few times a week, like a hunter-gatherer visiting known sources of nuts and fruit. I grazed the shelves looking for nutrition, and in the process bought a lot of books I may well never read.

In one of the better bookshops I found an old copy of one of the Novelist's novels, the one that had been pulped. When I next saw him he autographed it for me. I felt that in some way we had brought it back to life.

CABINET

THE FRENCH chargé d'affaires hinted to the Chinese that a live Milu specimen would be considered a great gift to the West. Since the current emperor was less than sixteen, it was up to the dowager empress to decide whether a deer should be given or not. She took an interest in the Lazarist school, and when she heard about Père David's *cabinet de curiosités* demanded that it be brought to the Forbidden Palace for her to see.

The cabinet contained, among other stuffed and mounted rarities, a section devoted to bizarre animals: a tortoise with green hair sprouting from its shell, a one-horned gerbil with powerful hopping legs, and a goose embryo with a large barnacle growing on its back. All passed close examination as genuine animals. In fact, the green hair was a cleverly introduced parasitic marine weed, which had been cropped after it had grown onto the tortoise's shell. A skilled taxidermist had fixed a sheep's horn onto the stuffed head of *Dipus annulatus*, a long-legged species of Mongolian gerbil, turning it into a miniature unicorn; the barnacle "shellbird" was another test of the taxidermist's ingenuity, which used casein, dried albumen, to cover the join between shell and embryo. As Père David confided to his diary, "The Chinese are the cleverest frauds in the world."

The dowager empress liked the cabinet of curiosities so much that it was conveniently forgotten and never returned.

A month after the cabinet was moved to the palace, a live female deer was taken in considerable secrecy aboard a French steamer bound for Cochin China and home.

COMPETITION

SOON THE Germans heard about Milu. And the British. And the Italians. Before long there was a regular exodus of deer from the forbidden park. It became a measure of a country's status, whether it could bully the Chinese into handing over one of their prized Su Bu Xiang.

The scramble for the deer exactly mirrors the scramble for possessions in China. From 1860 onward, every country with a navy and some ambition wanted a piece of China. As the Chinese saying has it, "The melon was sliced."

(i)   Russia seized territory north of Amur.

(ii) Britain and France razed the Peking Summer Palace as a reprisal for Chinese brutality.

(iii) France occupied Annam.

(iv) Britain annexed Lower Burma.

(v) France annexed Lower Cochin China.

(vi) Russia occupied Chinese Turkestan.

(vii) Japan took the Liuchiu Islands.

(viii) Britain annexed Upper Burma.

(ix) France took the whole of what later became Vietnam, Cambodia, and Laos.

Every demand for territory met with grudging Chinese acquiescence, their hand forced by the gunboats anchored off the coast. Only the poor Italians met with a rebuff when they demanded Sanmen Bay in 1899. Without a Pacific navy it was all bluster, and after three months of being ignored by the Chinese authorities, they withdrew.

This successful face-off with the West prompted the dowager empress to step up her antipathy toward the foreign devils. Earlier that year she had been forced to host her first meeting with the wives of the foreign ministers. Now she announced that she found the blue eyes of foreign women disgusting, as they reminded her of cats, which she detested.

END

PÈRE DAVID was off on his travels again. This time across to Xian province in search of a great white bear. His persistence paid off yet again, and he was able to add another name to the books by finding the giant panda.

But his health was now starting to give way. Dr. Martin of the French legation was adamant. To stay any longer in China, with its extremes of climate, would kill him.

Père David took this news very badly. He had many more trips planned. But in some ways it must also have been a relief. When someone of reputedly strong health, like Père David, starts to suffer from repeated illness, there is often a psychological factor at work. Perhaps he really wanted to come home.

Père David returned to the Basque country, to Espelette, to the house of his birth, with a pet spider he had brought all the way back from China. He amused his nephews and great-nephews with this tame arachnid, which he kept tethered by a silk thread wound around its body.

Uprising

In 1899 Ernest "Chinese" Wilson, the Birmingham plant collector, was sent to the collapsing Celestial Empire to obtain a living sample of Père David's *Davidia involucrata,* the ghost tree or dove tree, which so far had resisted attempts to be grown in Europe. Wilson was armed with Wardian cases—closed glazed boxes in which living plants could be expected to live during the months of a sea crossing.

Wilson found the ghost tree in Ichang province, just as the Boxer Rebellion was getting under way. The Boxers had taken up the cause of the poorer Chinese, with their hatred of railways, church steeples, missionaries, and other foreign innovations. There had rarely been a worse time to be a foreigner in China, but Wilson survived by refusing to visit any towns. He stayed out in the fields and forests looking for plants.

KUNG FU

A PARTISAN IMPRESSION of this period can be gleaned from the classic Kung Fu movie *Once Upon a Time in China III*. I have to say it is a great movie, starring the incredible Jet Li and featuring an amazing fight sequence using wet towels, but it is not a hugely reliable source for the actual event. In common with most Chinese movies, the foreigners are portrayed as arrogant buffoons, which isn't helped by the poor stock of non-Chinese actors they have kicking around Hong Kong. In a way the Chinese are still refighting the Boxer Rebellion, just as the Americans refought Vietnam in the movies, providing endless opportunities to redefine defeat.

FIRE, PAPER, WATER

THE BOXERS took their name from an intercepted message between two members of a secret society known as the Fists of Righteous Harmony. The assumption was that the "fist" indicated skill at boxing. In fact, only a few members of each secret society practiced Kung Fu, or the "iron cloth shirt" *chi gong*, which was supposed to provide invulnerability to hard blows. In far more cases, the secret societies of that time were simply populist antiforeigner mobs capitalizing on the mystique of martial arts. Instead of a long apprenticeship, the Boxers would intoxicate themselves by whirling until a state of trance was achieved.

First came the chanting of the magic words, chanted from a scrap of paper, held under the breath; read from, if reading had been learned, or from memory otherwise. And after the chanting, the scraps of fur-edged yellow paper were eaten with all the saliva attendant on such gatherings of the ecstatic.

Then corybant Boxers would begin to swirl, red wristbands and head scarves flying, halberds like hedge-pruning hooks, eyes glassy before falling down in a trance.

The boxing master might then do tricks with his chaff-cutting knife, slashing his own arms and legs but producing no wounds. Needles would be passed through cheeks and tongues.

Sometimes sleight of hand and trickery were used. Sometimes a man in a trance simply does not bleed as much as a man in a normal state.

Invalids were brought out to be healed. The cure for insanity was to make a paper doll, stick a strand of the sick person's hair to it, and burn the thing. Then crack your whips, for all ghosts fear the crack of a whip.

The Plum-Scented Warriors, Big-Sword Society Members, Fists of Harmony and Brotherhood, meeting on the village green to learn the ways of the divine.

But always those scraps of paper, scratched by the local penman into an ideogram of survival. One scrap to be eaten before battle, another to be worn as hard *qigong*, a talisman against the musket ball and shrapnel of the foreigner.

If a boxing master wished to summon disciples he would burn a notice, inscribed with calligraphy, and the smoke of the burning letters would bring warriors running.

> *Let the judicial officer come to the spirit's place on the charm;*
> *The iron clan, the Kitchen God protect my body.*
> *Amida's instructions pacify the three sides;*
> *Iron helmet, iron armor, wearing iron clothes.*
> *A gold-topped bronze pagoda sealed with a rock;*
> *sword chops, ax slashes—I knock them away with one kick.*

In a reduced form, the ritual of writing and casting spells into fire remains in the West. Children still write a list for Father Christmas and send it with fervent hope up the chimney on Christmas Eve.

The Boxer magic was trance, spell, and fire; incantations and vows made after fasting; and avoidance of women and their pollution. There is no warrior caste on earth that does not suspect women of sabotaging its strength. The worst time is at the full moon; to look at a woman then, her face beautiful in the soft silvery light, would be the end of a Boxer's strength.

When Western women asked what they could do to help after the siege of Peking had started, they were told to "stay under the tables and washstands until the shooting stops." There was more to this than male chauvinism. Even the "enlightened" Westerners suspected that the presence of women was harmful in time of war, or rather, the presence of feminine energy, which was also in men, although necessarily suppressed. Water is feminine energy, yin energy. Fire is yang. War is big yang and fears extinction, dousing, by the yin force of women.

The Boxers decided the Peitang cathedral was protected by the malign energy of a thousand Catholic nuns—how else could it withstand attack after attack?

If a boxing master cut himself as part of a trance performance and there was a menstruating woman nearby, he might have great difficulty stopping his own bleeding.

In one divine hand pieces of paper and fire, in the other water and blood.

Boxers who wanted to destroy the foreign devils' "fire baskets," the wide-gauge steam trains that ran from Tientsin on the coast to Peking, first burned all the tickets. It was the first of many salutary shocks to the Boxers when they discovered that burning the foreigners' small paper spells was not enough to stop the smoke-breathing metal monsters. Later they simply ripped up the tracks.

And who were the foreign spellmasters? Morrison, with his dispatches for *The Times*, Sir Claude MacDonald, with his endless notes requesting more arms, more picquets, more sandbags sewn from silk, and more wooden tablets to cover loopholes. The writing of orders, memos, lists—the modern form of the spell.

The foreigners misunderstood the fire in the Hanlin Library. They called it cultural suicide. In fact, it was the Boxers sending the biggest spell of all into smoke for the ancestors to read.

Heaven brought forth ten thousand things in order to support man;
Man has not one thing to recompense Heaven.
Kill. Kill. Kill. Kill. Kill. Kill. Kill.

SIEGE

Never make a demand of the Chinese which is not absolutely just: when you must make a just demand, see that you get it.   —*Lord Elgin*

ON 20 June 1900, the Boxers had both the Chinese court and the foreign legations in their grip. The Chinese promised safe passage to the coast for the foreigners; and the Russians, French, Italians, Japanese, Austrians, and Americans were all in favor of leaving Peking. The British remembered the Indian Mutiny and were against any movement from the fortifiable legation buildings until reinforcements arrived. Only the German minister, Baron von Kettler, was determined to discover just what the Chinese had in mind.

Fulgent in the bright sunlight, the baron's Usher and Cole waterproof pocket watch, inscribed by his American wife *CK* inside the silver casing, read two minutes past ten in the morning. In fourteen more minutes he would be dead.

The baron snapped the case shut, click-click, with one efficient move that ended with the watch in the second pocket of his finely pressed waistcoat. He was sitting down. An impatient slap of the book in his other hand against the side of the palanquin signaled the four carriers to move off. The baron's sedan chair arose in small but perfect stately splendor, lifted by his handpicked coolies, hooded in scarlet and green to notify all of their ministerial status. Next, in strict accordance with protocol, his dragoman, Herr Cordes, was lifted, but jerkily, more like a camel arising. Cordes' usual carriers had mysteriously not been available, and four kitchen boys had taken their place. It would be a rough ride.

The baron revived the lit green cigar between his teeth with several precise puffs, took it out of his mouth to turn a page, and predicted to himself that they would be lucky to be back in time for dinner. This was no cause for regret. The urgency of the mission, which stirred what he felt to be his unstoppable iron will, was like a full stomach, better in fact, His eyes gleamed above wide whiskers and a faint dueling scar.

Herr Cordes was less sanguine. True, earlier missions about the fire-scarred streets of the city had met with glares and no action. But he felt in the dry deserted roads some sort of portent. The murder of the Japanese chancellor Sugiyama only days before was still on his mind. There had been reports of children playing with the dead body before Japanese Marines had carried it away.

Von Kettler's courage was a mixture of ire and physical fearlessness and it had served him well in the past. He also believed he was fair. Take the disgraceful reprimand he'd received from the other foreign ministers over beating that impudent Boxer boy. The boy had received his due punishment: 300 strikes with a thin bamboo. Von Kettler had studied such beatings carefully. A full Chinese-style punishment meant accurate and repetitive strikes to the crease just below the bared buttocks, hitting the same spot again and again. After 230 such blows the skin would be broken. By 300, the beating was down to the bone. Salt would be applied to the wound to slow the healing. If the beating was repeated each month, as many were, the man would be crippled for life. Von Kettler was no sadist: the strikes to the boy's behind were widely spaced, not concentrated, the skin marked but not broken. And the civilian-minded ministers feared reprisals so much they would not even visit the foreign ministry! Only he had the guts to do that.

He thought about his wife, and it unsettled him, which of course just angered him further. What had she said? Just "Don't go," with that stranded look in her eyes. He'd taken the gun to stop her from worrying, the tiny and quite useless Forehand and Wadsworth .32 "Terror" in its neat leather case. Von Kettler was well aware that its nickname was the "suicide special," but he did not tell his wife that. Her desperate manner was distinctly odd—

she did not even seem to care that he had armed himself. Normally she would have been soft, oversolicitous, feminine, encouraging. Like Cordes.

Protocol dictated that he refuse an armed guard. Seven sailors equipped with the latest Mauser Gewehr 98s—a 7.92 mm bolt-action firearm, considered by many to be the finest rifle in the world—were told to return to the German legation barrack room. Only the unarmed *mafoos*, ceremonial outriders, would accompany them. Prince Ching had guaranteed his safe conduct. To take an armed guard would be to slight the prince and negate the fine diplomatic point at stake. Von Kettler relished this world, the furthest reaches of diplomacy in the moments before it toppled into war. The rules were so very different, yet the requirement of nerve was the equal of war, and the need for judgment greater.

He had little doubt that the legations would be massacred by the mob if they attempted to leave for Tientsin. Chinese assurances about the protection of missionaries and converts counted for very little. But as a minister he was less vulnerable than a missionary. He could use his prominence to prolong the uncertain period between war and diplomacy, long enough, he hoped, to leave warfare to any advancing column from the treaty ports.

So there would be no bodyguard. The pistol was different. A minister was entitled to carry whatever he liked as long as it was hidden, though von Kettler had more faith in his fierce reputation than in a tiny American-made revolver.

Rounding a corner, he could see people gathering at one end of the boulevard, and along its length milled more people around food carts with ducks stretched brown in a line. Two children flew a hexagonal kite made of red paper. A woman feeding a baby looked at him with indifference. It was vaguely cheering to see the barbers trimming queues, Manchurian pigtails, along the Southern Wall.

He took an interest now in the crowd. It seemed to ebb and flow toward him like undecided weather, red banners and black writing. A crowd without personality.

He thought fondly about how his wife had annoyed him by making a reference to Nietzsche. What was his wife doing reading such deceitful immorality? How like a woman to fall for such tortuous arrogance!

The simple act of getting things done was what counted. The crowd got nearer and louder, until at its forefront he took notice less of the sight than of the sure knowledge that this man meant to harm him. What nonsense! But before that, for a hair's breadth, the dead certainty of the ending. Then the fear wiped away—this young soldier was no Boxer—he wore a mandarin's hat with a feather and an imperial button. There was nothing here to concern the German. Von Kettler pointedly ignored this young soldier holding a rifle, coming toward him out of the crowd.

The outriders started to circle, their ponies skittish. Cordes was irritatingly behind him. Cigar was out. "Cordes!" shouted von Kettler, losing his calm. The young Chinese soldier, with half his face in the sun, unshouldered his rifle, a German rifle, a tube magazine II mm Mauser, old but serviceable. As long as he had his rear sight calibrated to the maximum, he might miss. Chinese soldiers often set their gun sights to one thousand meters on the mistaken assumption that the bigger number equaled more power. At close range their bullets went too high. But this young man knew what he was doing, he had the imperturbability of a gamefowler, he knew his rifle. "Down!" von Kettler shouted, but the bearers began inexplicably to wheel, bringing into view a new flank of chanting crowds, much closer. "Sha! Sha! Sha! Death! Death! Death!" they chanted. He stood up to get out as the chair descended, wobbly, higher than he should be, catching the lip with his spotless English boot. First there was the noise of the crowd shouting, then there was a scrambling silence. He saw Cordes running in the opposite direction, deserting him. A pony reared up, blocking out the sun for a moment. Then Cordes fell, probably shot.

The last minutes: struggling up to get to the impudent man. Then reaching for the pistol case. Noticing that his killer was a mere boy. A sudden decision to rush the lad. Knowing with full certainty the bullet will hit.

The attentions paid to von Kettler allowed Herr Cordes, wounded in both thighs, enough time to escape and make his way back to the foreign legation.

Von Kettler's body would be returned to the German legation at the end of the siege in a dull black wooden coffin, high at one end like a Chinese junk. Inside he had been arranged so as to be still holding his book. There was no sign of his watch and its gold chain, and this upset his wife terribly.

As soon as the foreigners knew that an imperial bannerman, presumably under orders from Chinese authority rather than a secret society, had murdered von Kettler, they closed the gate to the legation. The siege had begun.

HANLIN II

IN THE British legation, the bell cast for Queen Victoria's Diamond Jubilee had already been the cause of several nasty ricochets from snipers' bullets. The bell rang only in times of emergency, and it was ringing now. It was the third day of the siege, and the Chinese were trying to burn the foreign devils out.

Thunderheads of smoke poured from the legation roof, which was not yet on fire, but behind it the Hanlin Academy, which housed the oldest and richest library in the world, was already burning like dry grass.

The wind was not propitious. It was a typical dry summer breeze from the north, driving the flames like a bellows into the British legation.

In summer, the wind never changed direction during the day. They could expect the worst.

Now the smoke was hotter, salt-and-pepper swathes that sucked the air out of the compound. Tung Fu-Hsiang's Muslims fired from the upper windows of the burning academy at the snaking human chain of children, ministers' wives, Chinese converts, and missionaries slopping water from hand to hand using everything from cloisonné vases to chamber pots. Soon the roar of burning wood and paper drowned out the recondite sounds of musketry. Boxers were running from courtyard to courtyard inside the academy, systematically setting fire to the entire complex of buildings. A hole had been punched by British Marines through the wall of the British legation, across the arm's width of alley and into the nearest Hanlin cloister. This was the water head, where a doomed attempt was made to put out the fire. All along the smoking northern walls of the legation, water scooped from the odiferous Jade Canal was splashed to stop the fire spreading further.

The proximate air was so hot that the hundred-year-old trees standing in the legation courtyard burst spontaneously into flames, like huge match heads.

Inside the library, the largest repository of unprinted manuscripts in the world, the celebrated Yung Lo Ta Tien encyclopedia was burning. This work, which ran to an incredible eleven thousand volumes, contained "the substance of all the classical, historical, philosophical and literary works hitherto published, embracing astronomy, geography, geomancy, the occult, medicine, Buddhism, Taoism and the arts." The ignorant young men from the countryside who started the fire perhaps had no idea what they were doing. Nevertheless, it was said to be the greatest act of cultural felo-de-se in the history of mankind.

The fire was gaining ground. The wooden walls were now cracking in the intense heat of a hundred thousand stacked and burning manuscripts. If the British legation fell, the whole siege would be over, and no man, woman, or child could expect quarter from the short swords and spears of the blood-seeking "Fists of Righteous Harmony."

There was one last hope. The wind. Children with smoke-blackened faces stared at the sky. Men working hard, shirts straining against their shoulders, would check every few minutes with a hastily licked thumb held out to one side. Like a gathering silence it descended on everyone to wish for the wind to change. High in the now burning towers of the academy, the long red banners of the Boxers began to lose shape, drop into the flames, catch fire, then lift again, but this time extending out to the east.

The prayers of the besieged had been answered. Even the old hands like Sir Robert Hart said how remarkably rare it was for the wind to change like that in June. Slowly the fire blew back on itself and, lacking fuel, began to go out. In the evening a few determined sinologues, including Edmund Trelawny Backhouse, rescued those few scrolls and smoldering volumes that still remained in the destroyed center of two thousand years of Chinese culture.

American Wives

THE BARON'S wife, Maud von Kettler, believed until the end of the siege, when her husband's body was returned in its coffin, that he was imprisoned and not dead. Perhaps this optimism kept her going throughout the fifty-five-day siege of the foreign legations by Chinese troops. The foreign men built barricades and fought off attack after attack. The women sewed sandbags and worked in the hospital.

✻   ✻   ✻

The Russians were the worst for biting through thermometers. Turn your back on a wounded man and if he was sick and a Russian he would try to touch a nurse's behind. If he was very sick and a Russian he would simply cackle and chew the thermometer in two, mercury flying into the startled man's beard like metal beads from a broken necklace.

A new procedure was needed at the women's hospital now that they were down to the last two thermometers. Part of the problem was the homemade gun, which fired shells filed down at the rim to fit the breech. Filing was not a job to be envied. When the gun fired it shocked everyone; it was a uniquely unpleasant noise, a roaring and grinding of old iron that connected to the nerves in your back teeth. Not like the maxim gun, which made the acceptable noise of hard wood rapping on hard wood.

To watch someone carefully as the thermometer did its job took time. The two instruments left were of thick glass and took five minutes to show a true temperature. A nurse was needed just to watch, and there was a shortage of nurses.

They were down to one clinical thermometer when Baroness von Kettler donated her own. It was a handsome model that registered in less than a minute, which was a great improvement. When not in use it rested inside a mahogany box. She had last used this fine thermometer to take her husband's temperature during a slight fever the previous autumn. In the end, it was the only such instrument to survive the siege.

As important as running the hospital was the manufacture of sandbags. During the fifty-five-day siege it has been estimated that 40,000 were made and used as fortifications around the legations. That's roughly 730 bags a day.

There were three hand-operated sewing machines in the chapel and two in the house of Mrs. Conger, wife to the American minister. The six women of the Conger household produced 1,500 bags in three days.

Stout materials were used at first, and those of a naturally camouflaged hue: gray canvas, burlap, buckram, and sailcloth; army blankets and cotton sheets made dirty with charcoal. But this was soon forgotten as more and more exotic fabrics became all that were available. Elegant silks and satins; figured goods; legation curtains and damask; rolls of fine black cashmere appropriated from an empty dry goods shop in Legation Street; bolts of muslin, lustrine, crinoline, and surah; linens, woolens, chiffons doubled and trebled, baldachin, dimity, and calico; velvet cut from chair covers, brocades, and bed linen; portieres donated by Mrs. Conger, velvets and satins from Maud von Kettler's wedding trousseau; grass cloth, moreen, cotton twill and fustian, corduroy and velveteen; felt, worsted, skirt lining, and the most exquisite silk underwear the Americans had ever seen.

Mrs. Conger even cut up the rolls of silk the Empress Dowager had presented to her the year before. Not to be outdone, Ethel MacDonald, wife of the British minister, gave up her silk from the king of Thailand.

And the colors! The patterns! Scarlet, vermilion, delicate green, kingfisher blue, lemon yellow, mustard, mauve, orange, purple, pink, and puce; check, tartan, print, paisley, and polka dot.

The Chinese troops watched as this earth-filled patchwork quilt grew to cover every gap in the walls, windows, and doors of the legation quarter. Flags of a thousand new nations sewn into bags of sand!

TRUCE

QUITE UNEXPECTEDLY, halfway through the siege, a truce was called by the besieging Chinese. Gunfire and shouting were replaced by silence. The Russians even stopped their repetitive chanting of "Kill the tortoise eggs," a deadly insult in China by reason of the supposed homosexual tendencies of the tortoise.

During the truce, the Empress Dowager sent creaking carts filled with watermelons for the relief of the ladies, but refused to send ice on account of the Boxers' terrible addiction to the stuff—sending ice would just inflame the "Righteous Fists" to yet more robbery and murder. A brief market was set up and a roaring trade in duck, goose, hen, and thrush eggs was done. Some refused this bounty from their oppressors, some believed it was poisoned. Others only risked melon rind, and even then only after it had been pickled into a chutney.

One night during the truce, those on duty were treated to a rare sight. At first it sounded like distant musket fire, but in fact it was fireworks. A hundred men in costume formed a carnival dragon. Excited boys threw firecrackers and Roman candles, which bathed the many-footed dragon in a golden rain of crackling light.

Then from the courtyard of a temple came thirty men dressed in spotless white, dragging the City God on his car, a bulbous-eyed lion painted scarlet and breathing fire. The men pulling the car intoned thanks or berated themselves for past misdeeds. One man had a huge abacus draped around his neck—a sign of false accounting; another wore brushes tied like stocks around his—this man had written falsehoods. Others tortured themselves with the more usual cangue, a device that from a distance bore a resemblance to a wooden lavatory seat around the throat, but it was heavy and no joke to carry for the eight or so hours of the march. One young lad following the procession was naked except for his black shorts. He had two oil lamps pinned to his breast flesh with S-shaped hooks and another one dangling from the thin skin of his forehead. Some had model bridges with figures fastened by points into the muscles of their upper arms; many had cut themselves with swords and were in a trance, like Boxers. But these were ordinary folk and not Boxers.

TIMING

INTERTESSELLATION OF the stars! Corruption of the Heavens! And now the turning-up of that watch.

Nakayama, half Chinese, half Japanese, who spent the entire siege roaming Peking avoiding detection by the Boxers and spying for his Japanese masters, was the man who located von Kettler's timepiece.

He found it in Hong's shop on Crooked Water Lane, in the area known for pawn shops, all with the large carved wooden dragon in green and gold over the doorway. Hong's differed in its extent, a labyrinth of narrow alleys winding through the mountain of antiques, glass display cases, cabinets with locked drawers, and long narrow display tables. Hong's shop was bigger than any other and he would pawn anything. Porcelain ewers, conches and censers, tripod vessels, dragon jars, and water droppers; a hypodermic syringe made out of two brass thimbles and a bit of glass tube; tall-necked stoneware vases, gilt bowls with peony scrolls, parcel-gilt silver cups, silver padlocks from the T'ang, silver coins and silver bottles made in Sian; a perfect ivory shovel, no bigger than a fountain pen, decorated in turquoise and coral, for the sole purpose of removing bird droppings from a cage; bronze mirrors, gold pedestal bowls, pottery camels the height of a small child, white porcelain spittoons, tomb guardians in stoneware, Siberian jade rings in the shape of *pi*, gold and silver needles for acupuncture and cautery, a fragment of five-colored silk damask; a pair of gold-filigreed glass snuff jars, still wrapped in blue silk and nestling in matching pear-wood boxes of beautiful simplicity; bone spatulas, red pottery amphoras and bowls, half rings made of white jade, tall *tou* beakers, Shang ritual goblets and bronze vessels ornamented with dragons; a silk-stringed *ku-ck'in* zither in black lacquer; an enameled silver fingernail guard five inches long; a jade ear scoop and various bronze tweezers, tattered mandarin plumes in peacock and blue argus feathers; stringless harps, brass bells green with age, faded silk portraits of a famous ancestor, geomantic compasses, optics ground from quartz and glass, an astrolabe made from whalebone, bronze incense holders, bronze lions, and a camphor-wood commode with inlaid mother-of-pearl. Then there were the rooms of furniture: dressers, ironwood chests, and low lacquer tables, pyramid clocks set to a twelve-hour day, and over-stuffed chairs carved in imitation of the French. One room was dedicated solely to the pawned footwear of prostitutes—tiny clogs and sandals made for bound feet. Another room was for weapons: swords, spears, lances, matchlock rifles, hexagonal-barreled pistols, and a small iron mortar from the twelfth century. Von Kettler's pistol had been there, a beautiful miniature in a leather case, but it was bought a day after his death by the emissary of some Manchu trader. The watch, however, remained. Inscribed *CK*, made by a British firm, Usher and Cole, priced at ten taels—bargain.

It was a miracle that Nakayama spotted the watch, but he did. As he always later said, "When things are needed they fly to hand."

Straightaway Nakayama noticed the time on the dial. Sixteen minutes past ten. He was a spy, he knew the significance of that. It was Kettler's death hour. Either the watch had been hit, perhaps by the very bullet that had killed the German, or the watch had stopped by coincidence.

Intertessellation of the stars! Corruption of the Heavens! That watch was either a sinecure for life or a death sentence.

There is no such thing as coincidence in the life of a spy. A coincidence is nothing more than a pattern misunderstood, an explanation, a clue that one is too stupid to see. Men who believe in coincidences sleep well at night and are murdered by the morning. *CK*, read the watch. There was no coincidence. If Nakayama handed the watch over to the German ministry, then he would be rewarded. If a foreigner found the watch after the siege, then Hong would have some explaining to do. He might even be severely punished.

"That watch," mused Nakayama. "Ah yes, that watch," said Hong, polishing his jewelry viewer with a soft cloth. "Before the foreign devils come you must sell that watch to me for, shall we say, twenty taels," said Nakayama, looking at Hong without blinking. Hong was a good agent, he knew how to cooperate. Besides, he had heard there were foreign soldiers marching from the sea to relieve the legations. Everyone knew the Boxers had lost. He flipped open a cloth-covered box, which contained his ledger. "The man's name is Fu, but it is really En Hai," he said, looking up.

Several weeks after the siege ended, Lance Corporal En Hai of the Peking Field Force spoke before his decapitation: "I obeyed the orders of my superiors, otherwise why should a small person like myself venture to take the life of so exalted a personage as the German minister? My officers offered a reward of seventy taels and a promotion, but I only received forty taels, and waiting around in Peking for the promotion has cost me my life! I curse the bones of those princes who trapped me thus!"

An expiatory memorial was raised by the Chinese on the spot where von Kettler had been murdered. Strangely, the German inscription was removed after a few years and the white marble arch suffered a complete change in reputation. It became known among the Chinese rickshaw drivers and shopkeepers as the monument to the Boxer who had given his life to kill the foreign devil invader.

EXTINCTOR,
EXTINCTEE

THE CARVE-UP of China led to the death of the Celestial Empire and the extinction of a way of life that had survived for several thousand years.

But the dispersal of Pere David's deer throughout Europe had the very opposite effect. It stopped an extinction. The very greediness and competitiveness of the many nations involved meant a bigger gene pool of European Milu. In fact, it could be said that the nations were not greedy enough. Imagine if they had spirited away several hundred Pere Davids for their private enjoyment in Europe's capitals. Then the survival of Milu would almost have been guaranteed without Russell's involvement.

What can be said is that Russell was the only one in the chain of Milu's saviors who knowingly acted to save the deer from extinction.

With the benefit of hindsight, we can also applaud the first unknown emperor, Père David, and the various European diplomats in Peking in the nineteenth century. But at the time they didn't know what they were doing. They acted without knowledge—we can guess that from their later actions. Père David did not set up a deer park in France, and neither did the greedy diplomats, even though it must have been obvious that the deer were at risk from living in only one location—any reader of Darwin would appreciate that.

The idea of extinction had yet to sink in. It was events like the end of the Celestial Empire, and more crucially its age-old way of life, diced up by nations armed with guns and railway trains, which made extinction suddenly an observable event.

DEEP TIME

GEOLOGISTS AND paleontologists have a term for the eons of time needed to explain evolution. They call it *deep time.* The key thing about deep time is that it is unimaginable, not on a human scale. Compared to human time, deep time is infinite. It becomes a play area for scientists who no longer have to be embarrassed about the yawning million-year gaps in the fossil record. The gaps now become a strength. Instead of an implausible story about, say, fish evolving into humans, scientists can concentrate on establishing relationships between the few fossils they can actually lay their hands on. Without the need to stick to a centrally agreed-upon story, anything becomes possible. In the inconceivably lengthy deep time, whole species could have arisen and disappeared without any record: unicorns, for example.

Deep time seems to correspond to the infinite time of the

Zoroastrians, the time before humans began living in human time. According to Zoroastrianism, this was twelve thousand years ago.

The story of evolution, which has, in most places where people study science, replaced the Book of Genesis, tells of how a simple creature became a more complex creature, how an uncouth non-tool-user became a Victorian engineer.

Of course, this isn't the "real story" of Darwin's *Descent of Man*. The real story is incredibly complex and probably only understood by those who have devoted a lot of time to reading Darwin.

But we don't live our lives by real stories, at least not if they are complicated and tedious. We live our lives by cartoons, sound bites, simple stories for a brain that will always choose dramatic impact over truth. Every time. Almost every time.

The simple story says that might is right. That "progress" is inevitable. And the subtext is: if you're a freak, or a gypsy, or homosexual, or decadent, or disagree with me, or are just different in some way, then you deserve to die. In fact, we're doing nature a service if we help along your extinction, because nature means evolution, and evolution means progress.

But the scientists who espouse deep time, and its allied methodologies, make no such connection between evolution and progress. All they acknowledge is that organisms evolve. To make up a story explaining the path of that evolution is no longer considered credible science. There is simply not enough evidence to support fabulation. In the past, such fabulation depended for its credibility on the status of the fabulator, a literary judgment rather than a scientific one.

It's actually surprising that we've been taken in by these fables of prehistory for so long. They're so incredibly *thin*, like postulating the existence of Troy when you find a single brick.

Imagine if, in the far distant future, all evidence, both written and visual, were destroyed, except two photographs, one of Père David and the other of Herbrand Russell. If these were the only two photographs, people would feel duty bound to make up a story connecting them. And without knowledge of Milu, every story would be false.

If the huge swathes of time cannot support a story—and by a story I mean something exciting, like the dinosaurs dying out because an asteroid fell to earth—then all we can do is look and describe what is in front of our eyes. Measure bones. Compare one fossil with another.

You see how unbearable that is. How killjoyish. You can see why proponents of deep time are regarded with suspicion. In the name of truth, they are attacking our fundamental human need for stories.

DIARIES

Diaries are so often a medium for what was not said
or what cannot be said.   —*Paul Verlaine*

I N LIU-LI-CHANG, the street of booksellers, forgeries were easy
to come by. Written in an indecipherable "grass hand," they
relied on broken seals and stamps of high officials for their
authenticity. It was here that Sir Edmund Trelawny Backhouse
bought the diary of Ching Shan for one hundred taels, less than
fifteen pounds. Written on the instruction of Jung-lu, in order to
exonerate him in Western eyes and benefit his family after his
death, the diary is perhaps the most influential forgery in history,
rivaling the Protocols of the Elders of Zion.

The Ching Shan diary is still the basis for most interpreta-
tions of what was going on inside the Forbidden City during the
siege of the legations. The dowager empress is confirmed as a not
unsympathetic character. She, and the system she represents, is
shown as being able to control, to some extent, the destructive
urges of the Boxers. In other words, the diary confirms that the
decadent order of the day was not seriously challenged by the ide-
alistic Spirit Boxers. This view was forcefully represented by Morrison, and became the standard British Foreign Office line. It was

later to result in the consistent underestimation of that other idealist group, the Chinese Communist Party.

A completely different history might have awaited the Celestial Empire if the Communists had been recognized as a serious force and dealt with before achieving the kind of grassroots support that the Ching Shan diary emphasized was unimportant in China.

(In 1951, the Chinese Communist collection of documents concerning the Boxer Rebellion, the I Ho T'uan Tzu Liao Ts'ung K'an, quoted the Ching Shan diary as genuine, except that now it served the purpose of showing the decadence of the old order.)

Backhouse admitted in 1943, just before he died, to his Swiss friend Dr. Hoeppli, that "*I* did not falsify it." Untrustworthy though he undoubtedly was, if he was referring to the actual script, then he may have been telling the truth. Backhouse habitually made mistakes in writing Chinese characters, and the Ching Shan diary, for all its faults, has not been challenged for its calligraphy. Even if he dictated it, Backhouse did not write it.

What no one can really bear is that neither Westerners nor Chinese have any idea what was going on in the Forbidden City during the siege. It's a black hole in history, and that makes everyone uncomfortable.

The contrast between the number of "true" eyewitness accounts that came out of the siege on the foreigners' side and the paucity on the Chinese side couldn't be greater. On the face of it, the Chinese appear to be the callous disregarders of truth—after all, what have they to hide? The foreigners blurt it all out; their conscience is clear. But a real regard for truth means using it sparingly.

Meyrick Hewlett, who survived the siege as a student inter-
preter, remarks in his memoirs that a coolie repeatedly lied when
asked for his account of a petty crime he was involved in. Finally
the sheer quantity of his lies caught him out. Then he confessed
the truth. Asked why he'd held out for so long, he replied, "The
truth is very valuable—you can only use it once."

Since we can only provide approximate stories about the past,
every account is more or less a fake. Since our personalities are
not one but many faceted, any author is operating under a pseudonym. It is not a question of whether a diary is faked or not,
but whether we should pay heed at all to so many pieces of
paper.

In the years after the Communist takeover, the people of
Peking became used to a new sort of truth, something the Russians had taught the cadres. Suspects would be questioned
about their past endlessly—names, dates, places, people. Since
everyone is guilty of being an individual rather than an emana-
tion of the state, everyone is guilty of something. Attempts to
cover up would be doggedly sniffed out, contradictions would
be seized upon, used as a wedge to split open a harmless testi-
mony. In the modern state, the "truth" becomes a weapon of
repression.

BACKHOUSE

BORN IN 1873 and educated at Winchester and Oxford, Edmund Trelawny Backhouse was already bankrupt with twenty-three thousand pounds of debts by the time he was twenty-three. Three years later he popped up in China with letters of recommendation from then Prime Minister Lord Salisbury and Colonial Secretary Joseph Chamberlin. Coincidentally, Backhouse was distantly related to the 11th Duke of Bedford, Herbrand Russell, through a second cousin.

Backhouse arrived in China in 1898. It was a time of excitement and opportunity. Never had the Celestial Empire been so open to foreigners, backed up as they were by gunboat diplomacy and foreign troops based in the treaty ports.

Fortunes were being made. On the other hand, famine was a regular occurrence. In 1894 there had been both flood and famine near Peking on a scale larger than ever before. Whole sections of the Nan Haizi Deer Reserve wall were washed away and huge numbers of Milu escaped into the countryside. These were devoured by the starving peasants, for whom food was more important than conservation.

It was also a time of crisis for the dowager empress, T'zu-hsi. This former first concubine had outlived her emperor son and his

pregnant wife—the first a convenient death, the second a convenient suicide—had outmaneuvered the late emperor's legitimate
widow, and now outflanked her nephew, the docile Kuang-hsu,
emperor in name and nothing else. She had ruled since 1861 and,
with her Manchu relative and henchman Jung-lu, held onto power
using any means available. The Western powers, however, saw a
brighter future in supporting the weedy Kuang-hsu.

Incidentally, he was the last emperor ever to hunt Milu within
the Imperial Park. This was no small undertaking. At least two
thousand hangers-on would proceed with due ceremony to the
parkland, where a temporary pavilion was set up for the royal
entourage. Kuang-hsu loved to use his Schlesicky Strohlein binoc-
ular telescopes, with their revolutionary aluminum tubes and 16×
magnification.

The hunt was somewhat one-sided and, of course, the emperor
himself oversaw operations. A thousand halberdiers would move
in a line, rather like beaters rousing pheasants to be shot. The grazing Milu would then be driven toward the imperial dog-handlers,
who were clad in purple and controlled two packs of "lion dogs,"
surprisingly small terrier-type dogs that were capable, in a pack of
thirty, of bringing the largest stag down. Once a beast was isolated
and surrounded by barking dogs, the imperial hunters, also wearing purple, but with a green button on the chest, would move in
with their pikes and metal-tipped staffs. The stricken deer would
be speared in the lungs, tied to a staff, and stretchered off to be
butchered. Only the emperor was allowed to taste the meat.

As well as watching deer being killed, the credulous Kuang-
hsu, twenty-seven years old in 1898, was much influenced by the

Young China reform movement. This movement, which was based in Canton, was captivated by Western promises of wealth.

Modernization happened at a rapid rate in the 1890s. The old examinations in the Hanlin Academy were abolished. New tests in mathematics and science were instituted. Sinecures were forbidden in the "New Model" army. The fleet bought several French battleships before the dowager empress siphoned off the rest of the funds to rebuild the Summer Palace. Her sense of humor is apparent in the marble boat, reminiscent of a Mississippi paddle-wheel steamer, which she had built using money designated to buy real ships. Over eighty feet long, it is still "moored" in the palace lake.

But this act of profligacy was not a great triumph for the dowager empress. It became apparent to her and her Manchu kinsmen that they would be sidelined by the new reforms. Fortunately for the empress, a plot by Kuang-hsu to depose her was discovered by her loyal henchman Jung-lu. The emperor was arrested and forced to live under palace arrest on Ocean Terrace Island, in a lake by the West Wall of the Forbidden City. It is maintained that he was later poisoned on the orders of the dowager empress.

Initially, Morrison of *The Times* was impressed with Backhouse, considering him a useful and talented translator. Later he would revile him as a scoundrel.

During World War I, Backhouse acted as a secret agent for the British and was ordered to buy thousands of rifles and machine-guns for Kitchener's *matériel*-hungry New Army. He was pressed for results, but being unable to deliver he kept the money and pretended he'd been swindled by the Chinese. This became a pattern for extracting money from gullible foreign firms anxious to trade in China. Forged documents often supported his schemes. He'd learned the power of this with his forgery of the Ching Shan diary, which turned up in 1910 just in time to be useful as a central reference for the immensely influential book he cowrote with J. O. P. Bland, *China under the Dowager Empress.*

In later years, Backhouse became a recluse. One of the few people he conversed with was the eminent Peking-based Swiss physician Dr. Hoeppli. It was Hoeppli, in 1942, who encouraged him to complete his supposedly obscene memoirs.

DECADENCE

BACKHOUSE'S OBSCENE memoirs. I found the most sympathetic librarian I could. She knew nothing, but the word *Backhouse* rang a bell with the woman polishing the teapot behind her. Backhouse had just been photographed onto microfilm. I was in luck.

But I wanted the real thing, not some microfilmed copy. I agreed to try the microfilm, but it was, in places, impossible to read. I demanded the actual text. Everyone looked shifty. They knew it was pornographic. I knew it was pornographic. They weren't going to let it go without a fight. Eventually the chief curator was called.

Decadence Mandchoue came in a delightful blue-calico-covered box with interesting flaps and ivory securing pins. It was typed on thin U.S.-sized bond paper with a photo of Backhouse—white-bearded and slant-eyed, the left eye a little sleepy, eyebrows raised to induce a slight epicanthic fold, giving him the desired mandarin air. He was seventy-one.

Edmund Backhouse always remembered the dowager empress fondly. "I have sought to indicate her greatness even on occasions when dignity might have been dragged in the dust; as when she fondled the genitals of the princes of her clan or inspected the capacious anal cavities of pathic patricians and mimes."

I sat in the reading room, sneaking looks at the other readers, full of the childish joy of reading rude stuff when everyone else was politely studying dull and worthy tomes.

Backhouse had a sense of humor, of that there is no doubt, though it was largely missed by Hugh Trevor-Roper, the historian called in to verify whether the Backhouse memoirs were true or not. Trevor-Roper was later duped by the Hitler Diaries, of which he said: "I know his signature, I know Hitler's handwriting . . . the directors of *Stern* [who unearthed the diaries], one must assume, do not engage in forgery." Except they did. Or, rather, were eager to pay someone who did. Even though Trevor-Roper changed his mind a week later about the authenticity of the diaries, the fact remained: in the first instance he got it wrong.

Trevor-Roper had a hard job proving the inauthenticity of Backhouse's memoirs, because every event referred to has an alibi. Even Backhouse's first meeting with the dowager empress is covered. He returns cartloads of loot he saved after the relief of the legations—she is grateful and their intimacy proceeds apace. But

Backhouse realizes that these carts would have been seen by someone, so he sets the day of their delivery as that of the Peking horse races, which every single foreigner would have attended. A fortunate coincidence, but only a liar would draw it to our attention. His protests of innocence and his "alibis" would work in a conversation, momentarily glossing over the uncomfortable extravagance of his assertions. In print they soon become a screamingly obvious cover-up.

But there was no proof that Backhouse had lied. Any instinct for the truth has to be backed up by proof, or else we begin to doubt our own instincts. So we learn to trust proof rather than ourselves. Our instincts, like any unused skill, go into abeyance. Paradoxically, then, the Western obsession with evidence serves to undermine our own attempts to become sensitive to, and practiced at, discerning the truth.

After months spent unearthing scams and duplicities in Backhouse's eventful life, Trevor-Roper was even more convinced that Backhouse was a compulsive liar. The lies he told were well camouflaged, but eventually official documents showed up inconsistencies. Trevor-Roper at last had his proof. After a thorough perusal of Backhouse's "grotesque sexual obsessions," Trevor-Roper announced them to be "pure fantasy throughout." Trevor-Roper also disapproved: "No verve in the writing can redeem their pathological obscenity." This is prudery. The memoirs are designed to impress and amuse:

> At school, I recall how Winston Churchill, when being flogged, as very frequently occurred, would vociferate and flinch in coward poltroonery almost before he was hit; while other boys

(including myself) bore the chastisement without a groan or the least sign of flinching.

Or:

My bizarre affinities amused her [the dowager empress]; my homosexuality, amoral, totally uncurbed by ordinary standards, and its concomitant manoeuvres, masochismus, sadismus, pedicatio, fellatio, irrumatic, anal titillation and osculation, labial evolutions (as of a bacchanal or Menade), which some might not, ay, could not, savour, all these appealed to her temperament, as they assuredly did to Li Lien Ying [the chief eunuch], himself a would-be protagonist in such of my amorous "business" as (alas! in the scanty degree available to a eunuch's restriction) was feasible to him.

Or:

She [the dowager empress—who was in her seventies at the time] loved to pursue a sort of anal connexion with myself by means of her unusually long and erect clitoris, when she was not inserting her long-nailed index finger (at least four inches long) in my proctal cavity. It may be that other foreign devils would have hesitated to allow such liberties even from T'zu-hsi....

I was bunking off and knew it. Often I'd glance at my watch and make feeble resolutions about when I'd finish reading this filth and start in on the real research; which, of course, was vaguely elsewhere.

TRUTH III

PEOPLE USE different rules of thumb for guessing at the truth of a story. One is the boring = true, interesting = false school. The Hitler Diaries were tediously lacking in bedroom details about Eva Braun, and therefore were more likely to be true than a sexy romp through the wolf's lair.

If the truth really is dull, or too complicated, then a mendacious but exciting story will always displace it. That is the power of the Backhouses of this world. Our reaction in the West to this is interesting. It is to throw up our arms in dismay and to castigate the storytellers, the "frauds," as we like to call them.

Another reaction might be to use the experience to hone our ability to discern fact from fiction. Since truth survives not by telling truthful stories but through developing our instinct for the true.

PUB

K LAUDIA TELEPHONED and said that she would be passing
through Oxford on her way back from a literary festival. She
suggested that the Novelist and I meet her in "one of Oxford's
great little pubs."

It was a timeless summer afternoon, the kind of afternoon that
is done nowhere better than Oxford. I cycled down South Parks
Road to get to the King's Arms, past the big iron railings that
curve around the University Parks, the flowering trees spilling out
a civilized country feeling onto the dry gray tarmac along which
my wheels easily turned. Students walked under horse chestnuts
dark with foliage, which only recently had been bare branches.
Now there was a church-path dimness caused by leaves overbur-
dening ancient outward-leaning walls. And out of this dark tunnel
I bicycled into the puddle of light outside the pub, where a forgiv-
able mess of students crammed round two heavy bench-tables
with crisp wrappers tightly rolled and jammed into gaps between
the planks on top.

The Novelist was inside. He preferred inside. He particularly
liked a back room that was favored, I remembered from my student days, by codgers and odd dons, those with a drink problem.
Things had changed. Klaudia and the Novelist were in the nar-

row, dark, far end of the back room. Instead of the codgers, there was a table of seven girls penning them in. Getting a drink entailed pushing past this annoying table of seven giddy girls drinking pints of lager.

Since the Novelist was higher up the global pecking order than me, I sat meekly as he and Klaudia talked cryptically about his next novel. From what I could glean, I understood that the new novel might have something to do with Latvia; or perhaps not, since I knew that that was one country the Novelist had never visited. Post breakthrough, it would have to be mega to stop the inevitable backlash, but such thoughts were far from everyone's mind on that sunny afternoon.

I told Klaudia about the Pyrenees and Père David and she agreed I was on the right trail. She asked me when I was off to America, to the exotic game ranch. I said soon. "And China after that, I do envy you," she said. I signaled my agreement by nodding vigorously, though this wasn't exactly true. With our child about to be born, my mind was fully occupied—so fully occupied that I was hardly writing at all, and I couldn't even contemplate traveling to another country.

And I certainly didn't tell Klaudia my qualms, my darkest fears about the wall I kept circling and could never push through or see over. I knew even as I spoke that America and China were just so much more lateral movement, displacement, side stories. We want things to go forward, but history, I was learning, always went sideways.

I had hoped we could spend the afternoon like students, drinking and talking about all kinds of interesting things, but the Novelist had to do some research in the Bodleian for his new novel and Klaudia had to get back to her office in London. They left me on my own with a pint of Guinness, sun shining in through the tiny leaded windows and the giddy girls shrieking with laughter.

EGYPT V

WITH MY *gnawing hunger and a sense of growing defeat, I redoubled my efforts to find secondhand books. I did not believe the Lonely Planet guide. Somewhere in Egypt I knew there were books waiting for me.*

We made an excursion out to Fayoum, an oasis near Cairo, and it was there that I first heard about Ezbekiya Gardens.

We were visiting a friend of a friend, a famous film director who owned a Hasan Fathi–designed villa right on the lake at Fayoum. That's the good thing about Egypt—famous film directors don't hide themselves away. If you want to meet them, you can.

When we arrived I was glad to get out of the car. There had been four accidents on the desert road. Driving past one wrecked car I had seen something wrapped in torn newspaper. It was a dead body lying by the roadside.

The director made my wife a coffee in the little bare kitchen. The rest of the house was equally empty. There weren't even carpets on the cold stone floors. He sat in a soft black leather armchair and we sat on a soft black leather sofa, and that was about all the furniture in the whole place.

The director talked about making films in Egypt. He said that the real skill was being able to get a caterer who actually brought food, actors who actually turned up, a power supply that didn't pack up, lights that didn't blow. He said it had taken him fifteen years just to learn how to get things done. Compared to these skills, the artistic side was nothing.

I didn't want to comment on the lack of books, in case it sounded rude or high-handed. But in the end he brought the subject up himself.

"I don't have any books, you can see. That way, if I'm raided they haven't got anything on me. It's all in here," he said, tapping his graying temple.

I knew the director had been in prison briefly during Sadat's clampdown in the early eighties, but I thought he had long given up Communism. He drove a new BMW, owned a holiday villa, and directed films that were released on the commercial circuit.

"Do you fast?" I asked.

He laughed. "Only when I have guests. I'm not religious."

Now I understood. He didn't fast, so he didn't need books. We talked about my insatiable need for reading material, and that's when he mentioned Ezbekiya Gardens. He explained that it had been the site of a huge book market somewhere in downtown Cairo.

"But that shut down," my wife said, "years ago."

The director nodded. We all agreed it was a terrible pity.

"The largest secondhand book market in Egypt?" I asked the director.

"Maybe in the entire Middle East," he said.

ENCYCLOPEDIC

MORE DEVIATIONS. I checked the computer, and after the usual false starts, I found the list of Chinese books and manuscripts donated by Sir Edmund to the Bodleian. These included volumes of the Yung Lo Ta Tien encyclopedia that he had pulled from the burning Hanlin Library a hundred years ago. I ordered up the original manuscripts of the greatest encyclopedia the world has ever known.

The Yung Lo Ta Tien (or as some prefer to render it into English, the Yong-le Da Dian) encyclopedia was designed to cover all knowledge at the time it was written, and not just in synopsis—entire books and sizable verbatim extracts formed the substance of this encyclopedia.

The arrangement of the texts within conformed to a poetic rather than a mechanistic system. The first word of each text quoted was ordered according to the fifteenth-century rhyming dictionary Hong-Wu-Zheng Yun.

The origin of the encyclopedia was magnificent. The third Ming emperor decided to preserve all known literature. At first, 147 scholars were set to work. But ten years went by with only modest results. In 1404 the emperor appointed 2,169 more scholars to work for seven more years to complete the project. The seventy conservators at the British Library look piffling by comparison.

By 1408 it was ready. Years later many lost works could only be found in the Yung Lo Ta Tien. It was too huge ever to print, being composed of 11,095 large volumes executed on fine white paper ruled in vermilion and bound in hard boards covered with yellow silk.

Today there are only 370 volumes left. Two hundred or so remain in China and the rest are scattered around the globe. The Bodleian has nineteen volumes, eleven donated by Backhouse.

The volumes that I looked at in the Bodleian are not the first edition—these were destroyed in another fire in 1744. Fortunately, a copy had been made in the preceding century. One hundred scholars working full time for five years had produced this one copy between 1562 and 1567.

By 1773, 2,273 *juan,* or chapters, were recorded as missing from the great encyclopedia. There were roughly two chapters to a volume, so roughly a tenth of the corpus had already been pilfered. This steady decline continued into the nineteenth century. No one knows how many volumes were burned in the fire, but we can be sure the Yung Lo Ta Tien was far from complete at that date.

I was surprised at how modern the sixteenth-century volumes looked. Rebound in blue boards to replace the original imperial-yellow silk, they looked as if they were less than a hundred years old. There was no foxing or yellowing and the paper was still pliable and tough. Comparing the volumes, I could see how styles varied ever so slightly depending on who had been the copyist at the time.

The volumes were of large format but were only about seventy or eighty pages long. I counted the characters—there were about five hundred per page. Very roughly, then, each volume was about forty thousand words, slightly less than this book you're reading. The entire encyclopedia would have had the same word count as the stock of a large secondhand bookshop.

LOOT

E BONY AND wax seals broken on the foot-long brass lock, Mrs. W. P. Ker, a survivor of the siege of the British legation, entered the private apartments of the empress at the Ming Shou Palace. She was the first female sightseer after Cossack troops had secured the outer gates of the Forbidden City.

Looting had already taken place. Obscene scrawls in barely decipherable Cyrillic were scratched into the wall-high camphorwood boxes in the dressing room.

This was mild indeed. All were now familiar with disquieting gossip concerning Marshall Count von Waldersee cavorting on an imperial divan with a pliant Chinese prostitute while his soldiers methodically looted the place. In the Summer Palace, the empress's golden phoenix throne had been unceremoniously chucked off the

Peony Terraces into the Lake of the Western Hills. "Lewd and ribald drawings and writings" were scrawled by Russian conscripts on every available wall. Meanwhile, the French helped themselves to the Louis XIV instruments, ground lenses in golden settings, gifts from one Sun King to another, that had lain unused in the Imperial Observatory since the inauspicious reporting of a comet in the months before the Boxer uprising. But everyone agreed, and *The Times* reported as much, that the worst and most systematic looting was by the Germans.

That said, Morrison, chief correspondent of *The Times*, did manage to help himself to the entire contents of a wealthy Chinese prince's house, even down to the flowering shrubs in the garden. "I have left him the glass in the windows, but nothing else." This was despite a suppurating gunshot wound in the journalist's thigh. Had he been fit, Morrison announced that with his exceptional local knowledge he would have been richer in plunder than even Lady MacDonald, wife of the British minister Sir Claude, who, with a small, well-armed force of Marines, "devoted herself most earnestly to looting."

What everyone was ultimately after was the fabulous wealth of the Celestial Empress. The Germans were the most systematic, and before the Russians secured an international agreement that the Forbidden City should remain untouched, they had searched every cellar and attic for the dynastic wealth of the Manchus.

Later, and despite the agreement, a Russian, General Lineivitch, returned to his post in Amur loaded with ten chests of silk, fur, and ormolu valuables from the royal apartments. In this bout of looting, the indefatigable limping Morrison made off with the dowager empress's jade prayer tablet from the camphor-wood escritoire at her bedside. But no one found the treasure.

Mrs. Ker, in her visit, could have helped herself had she but known the secret of the empress's bedchamber. Past the embroidered coats of black satin set with pearls, the Manchu shoes, and the boxes of silk handkerchiefs, overturned, some pale yellow, some pale blue; past dressers filled with sable skins and silk coats lined with fox, carved rose and sandalwood screens; past chairs and stools of jade and lacquer, jewel-trees, porcelain vases of celadon and *"sang de boeuf"*; past all this; past even the room of foreign clocks, "some handsome, others hideous, all ticking cheerfully, regardless of the ominous silence around . . ."

Even the eunuch who wound the clocks did not know the secret. The treasure was not buried beneath the city, though some valuables were interred under the paving flags of the Palace of Peaceful Old Age. Nor was it hoisted into the pagodas above the simmering confusion of the Chinese court. No thickened walls or massive locks protected the imperial wealth from foreign hands. No strongbox or patent safe but rather a flimsy screen of silk. Using the same trompe-l'œil that hides the doors to the Dagoba behind the Buddha in a Chinese temple, a silk partition in the dowager's bedroom gave the illusion of a solid masonry wall. Behind the silk, undisturbed until her return, "lay all the gold and jewels" of China.

BOOKS OR ANIMALS?

THE FIFTY-FIVE-DAY siege ended when an army of Russians, Japanese, Italians, and British, including Grandpa Tom, marched into Peking. Chinese troops fought briefly before being overwhelmed by the foreign armies. The occupying force stayed on in Peking for many months, and food was in short supply.

Père David died on 10 November 1900, just after the relief of the foreign legations in Peking. I like to conjecture that just as the last deer was slaughtered by a hungry Russian soldier camped in the imperial deer reserve, so Père David keeled over and died. I mean, it's possible, isn't it?

Long-dead empires are remembered by the things they built and by the books they wrote that we are still able to read.

It struck me then that perhaps Père David did not die when Milu was killed off in China. There were still, after all, examples of the deer in Europe. Perhaps he died when the library had been burned down, when the original information about Milu was lost. The Hanlin Library was destroyed on 23 June 1900. Père David died five months later, in Paris, after several months of illness. Perhaps the onset of that fatal illness coincided with the fire? It's a poetic conceit, but in my mind I cut the two sequences together—Père David dying and the library burning down. I thought about all the plants and animals named after him, how his contribution had been not to nurture living things but to kill things and record things in books. In a real sense Père David cared more for books than for animals.

EGYPT VI

M Y WIFE *said they paved over Ezbekiya Gardens with concrete, and that's why the booksellers left. I wasn't satisfied. Everyone I met I questioned about Ezbekiya Gardens. My wife's aunt thought the Ezbekiya booksellers had moved to Hussain. Hussain is the area near Khan al Kalil, which the Lonely Planet writer called "The Khan," after the manner of "The Hood." Khan al Kalil is the bazaar where every tourist goes to buy knickknacks. It is also the area made famous by the novels of Naguib Mahfouz. But behind the bazaar for tourists is a bazaar for everything else you could possibly imagine. Because of its winding alleys and crowded streets, I love going to the place. It feels like a real bazaar, unlike the antiseptic grand bazaar in Istanbul. And though the government is always threatening to demolish it and replace the original inhabitants and their houses with a folkloric shopping center, they haven't done it yet. Surely no government could be so stupid as to get rid of a prime tourist site?*

Hearing about Ezbekiya Gardens made me change my mind. If they could get rid of a place where secondhand books were traded, they could get rid of anything. By now I had gleaned more information from Nadim, an Egyptian psychiatrist who lived in the Arctic Circle in Canada but was back for a holiday.

Nadim outlined the many advantages of living inside the Arctic Circle if your profession is psychiatry. For a start, no one wants to work there, so you get a big bonus incentive from the Canadian government. Secondly, there is no shortage of patients—those depressed by the twenty-four-hour darkness of winter and Eskimos suffering from extreme alienation provide a constant source of revenue. Thirdly, the lack of other psychiatrists means the government does not restrict how and when you work. You can work all round the clock if you want, seeing patients at 11 P.M.

Nadim was there simply to make money. He was very sane about the whole thing. He was also very informative about Ezbekiya Gardens, since he often went there as a boy. He told me his family used to stroll around the gardens on summer evenings.

The only time I had actually seen the place was from a speeding car shooting along a flyover that crossed the gardens far below. Beneath the sooty ramparts of the bridge I glimpsed more roads, traffic, modern buildings in a semiderelict state, and people in rags riding on donkey carts loaded with garbage. No greenery, though.

Nadim told me the gardens were now a small, enclosed area. The lake had been filled in and the opera house had been burned down by supporters of Sadat, shortly before he took over from Nasser.

"But Sadat was in favor of modernization and Western influence— why would his supporters burn down the old opera house?" I asked.

"That was why they burned it down," said Nadim. "They wanted to show the middle classes that nothing was safe and that it was necessary to support Sadat in his political clampdown."

Nadim and his brother used to wander around Ezbekiya Gardens looking *for books in French and English. The booksellers used to lay their wares out in piles on the wide pavements. There were hundreds of sellers, said Nadim, and thousands of books. "You could get anything in Ezbekiya Gardens," he said with some warmth. "And for almost nothing, because foreign books were seen as worthless. My brother found a first edition of Victor Hugo for fifty piastres!"*

Strong stuff for a bookhead like me.

I went to Hussain with my wife to try and find the displaced booksellers of Ezbekiya Gardens. We found some bookshops, but they only sold books in Arabic and religious books. It seems that my wife's aunt had been wrong.

Ezbekiya Gardens became a symbol for me of all that was good about the past, and its destruction now meant something very bad indeed. But where had the books all gone? You can't just abolish a book market overnight, not the biggest in the Middle East, surely?

"Why not?" said Nadim.

"All those books must have gone somewhere," I said. "They must be somewhere here in Cairo, maybe in a warehouse or something."

Nadim shrugged. I supposed that living in the Arctic Circle had made him more open to anything being possible. A huge book market could disappear if the property developers and their government lackeys decided it would.

Nobody I asked about the disappearance of Ezbekiya Gardens thought it meant anything more than "progress." Everyone accepted that there would be more cars and more crummy apartment blocks and that that was the price you paid for having electric gadgets and better health care, for "progress."

What struck me as extraordinary was the deep belief that you had to have either one thing or the other. You couldn't have medicine and gadgets without every garden being turned into a twenty-story building. Everyone was fatalistic about this. Everyone instinctively knew that something out of control was at work, a monster that gave us sweetmeats—if we wanted the sweetmeats we had to tolerate the monster.

Humans have always tolerated monsters. But this one had no face, was intangible, not even formally agreed upon.

The cars were getting to me now. On my first few visits to Cairo I had found the traffic exhilarating. There were a lot of cars, but they always seemed to be moving. If you were in a taxi you were always going somewhere. Increasingly, though, I found it quicker to walk through the fume-laden streets than to sit in a cab in a traffic holdup. And the cars were less interesting, modern Japanese cars, the same the world over.

But even in a traffic jam you'd see interesting things. A bicycle with a steering wheel instead of handlebars. Two men slaughtering a sheep by the roadside. An astonishingly beautiful beggar girl with a crutch and a lame leg and a scowl. Four men rebuilding an engine on a traffic island. Human stuff, better than television.

In fact, one day, a cab driver I'd become friendly with wedged a TV between the front two seats of his Polski Fiat cab for me to watch as we drove. Apart from the poor reception and low quality of Egyptian TV, I still wasn't interested. Even if I had been facing the best Hollywood movie on a perfect screen, I would have been looking out at the street. In Egypt, critical mass has not been reached—life is still more interesting than television.

But with Ezbekiya Gardens gone, how long would that last?

FARM PLAN

M<small>Y MOTHER</small> rang and told me that the farm where she had grown up and where Grandpa Tom had lived in his caravan was coming up for auction. She was going to have another look around the place. "If I win the lottery this week," she said, "I'll buy it back."

The reserve price was a million pounds, twenty times the fifty thousand my family sold it for in 1968. My grandfather had bought the farm in 1940. Since my aunts and uncles weren't interested in farming, my grandfather had felt duty bound to sell it, at less than market price, to the grandson of the man he'd bought it from. But now the grandson was old, and none of his daughters wanted the farm either. He had a bad back, and most of the land was used as a holiday caravan site, making use of its nearness to Stratford-upon-Avon.

Now no one, on either side of each family, wanted to carry on farming—not unless we won the lottery, that is.

When Grandpa Tom lived on the farm, his was the only caravan. Dark green, not dissimilar to the one Monty ended his days in.

I can actually only remember Grandpa Tom speaking about sixty words. We visited the farm regularly, but he spoke rarely. As a result, the only solid connection to the Boxer Rebellion was his handing round of the photograph of the severed heads in the street. He would pass it round silently, and my father would fill in the historical facts.

Grandpa Tom never spoke about any war that he had been in. He survived the whole of the first war as an infantry private, but his medals remained wrapped in their issue envelopes inside his portable desk-box.

His interests when I was young were walking very slowly to the big road and finding things on the footpath by the canal. He often found wallets and dropped coins. In his box he had an 1860 farthing and a rare penny from 1912.

When he discovered that I collected the tight rubber bands used to make lambs' tails drop off, he used to give me any he found while out walking.

UNICORN

THE CHINESE unicorn, *ch'i'lin*, was anciently described as having the body of a deer, the tail of a cow, and the hooves of a horse. From the Han period it was believed to be a benevolent animal, whose fleshy horn equipped it for war, although it never did harm.

The implacable T'ang dynasty skeptic, Wang Ch'ung, declared that just as the serpent turns into a fish and the mouse turns into a turtle, so the stag is transformed, in times of peace and tranquillity, into a unicorn.

Milu's antlers look reversed because the brow tine, the forward antler prong with no "points" growing off it, is absent. Instead, the position occupied by the front prong is taken by the blades and spikes of the main part of the antlers. And sticking out at the back is a rear-facing prong or tine.

When antlers are growing, their nurturing "velvet" would make them appear fleshy.

From a distance, the bulk of a young Pere David's antlers would appear as one, the rear tine blending in against the thick neck, perhaps.

Milu was described as having the head of a deer, the hooves of a cow, the tail of a mule, and the neck of a camel.

In fact, the hooves are distinguished by the clicking noise they make. Only reindeer make the same noise with their hooves. Milu's feet are well splayed and good for keeping a footing in a marsh.

From a second-century A.D. wooden carving of a unicorn excavated at Wu-wei in Kansu province, it is possible to note the prominent hooves, erect tail, and heavy shoulders. The single horn has the sweep of a straightened and lengthened bull's horn. The inspiration seems half bovine, half ungulate. The flesh of Milu is supposed to taste similar to beef and venison.

The appearance of unicorns in the empire was a good portent, deserving an immediate report to the emperor. The bearer of such news could expect a reward in "shoes"—ingots of silver and gold.

The scarcity, if not actual extinction, of Milu in the wild over the last thousand or more years parallels the elusiveness of the unicorn.

Ch'i'lin was also used metaphorically to mean a great genius, a symbol of success in the scholar-official's career.

There is no provable connection between the Chinese and the Western heraldic unicorn.

CALF DEATH

M Y INVITATION arrived from Woburn in an expensive-looking cream envelope. I was invited for a day and a night in order to reconnoiter the place and to meet the librarian, the archivist, and Callum the deerkeeper.

I wondered if I might by chance meet the world's expert on Milu, Maja Boyd, at Woburn. She hadn't replied to the letter I'd sent to her in China, so perhaps she had left that country and was visiting England.

Lord H's family had been very kind to Maja Boyd, even providing her with a free apartment to live in on the estate whenever she wanted to view her beloved Pere Davids. If, and I knew this was fairly unlikely, I was offered a free apartment, I made up my mind definitely to take it.

Callum was a Scot. I met him at the estate office as soon as I arrived at Woburn. He drove me in his Land Rover to see the

Pere David herd. This was my first in-the-flesh viewing of Pere Davids, and given that I had been building up to this moment for six months, I was glad not to be disappointed. I was happy that each part of the deer really did look mismatched: the neck is thick and shaggy as a camel neck is, the tail does swish like a horse's tail, and the feet have a hoofiness that is definitely more bovine than ungulate. The deer really had the four characteristics that do not match—and when you see them alongside other deer, the backward-pointing antlers shout at you to be twisted forward.

The older males grazed separately from the younger males and the females, who were coming to the end of the calving season. Callum pointed out that the females ran a crèche system, two being assigned at any one time to guard the eighty or so new calves.

Scanning the herd with the Zeiss 8×30s (definitely the business as far as deer management goes; I resolved to get some as soon as I got a big enough advance against royalties), Callum noticed something wrong. "That female over there," he pointed. "Looks like she's in pain."

We rumbled slowly forward in the Land Rover. The rule with deerkeeping is: Don't walk when you can drive. And though the deer must have known that the vehicle contained humans, they were more wary of us when we got out than when we were inching forward in crawler gear.

The female was staggering. "Can you see that hanging out of her behind?" said Callum. I could. The tips of a calf's hooves. Callum explained that the calf would now be dead; lying in the wrong position in the womb, it had failed to be born. "The mother will be in agony," he said, "and will die in a day or two."

He picked up the crackly walkie-talkie from the dashboard. "Bring your gun," he advised his assistant.

Things were going a bit fast for my liking. I'd only just been introduced to the herd and we were about to take a pop at them. I'd thought the killing would come much later, if at all.

Callum explained that the herd are kept in semiwild conditions. They aren't interfered with in any way, except to receive extra feed if it's a hard winter. The vet isn't called, because the Pere Davids either get fatal diseases or they recover on their own. The deer certainly aren't mollycoddled with antibiotics and other man-made products.

"Their meat must taste really good, being pure and everything," I said.

"Oh, it does," said Callum. "Somewhere between steak and venison—delicious." Part of the reason, no doubt, that the Emperor of China had hogged them all for himself.

The assistant rolled over the parkland toward us in his Hi-Lux pickup—the alternative vehicle for the committed country lad. Not that I'm into vehicles, but in the country it seems that you're either a Hi-Lux man or a Land Rover man. Ray Mears, the survival expert, had a Land Rover like Callum. Land Rovers are definitely less showy and more patriotic—real Land Rovers, I'm talking here, not office-girl Discoveries or that new one that looks like an orthopedic boot.

I could see the rifle poking out of the Hi-Lux side window. Callum told me it was a Sako .243; a top professional rifle, he said.

The gunshot sent a shockwave of noise through everything. The deer was down instantly. We roared up in our vehicles. She kicked and shuddered and died. It was a clean head shot. The hooves of the dead calf protruded from her wet-haired hindquarters. Some blood, not buckets. The carcass was damn heavy, I could see, but I did not help as the others hauled it by the legs onto the low-loading trailer behind the pickup.

SUNRISE

LATER THAT day I drove up to the abbey, the big house in the Woburn grounds, ready for my first taste of country-house living. There were no Rolls-Royces and Mercedes parked outside, just ordinary cars, and mine did not look out of place. Maybe they were the servants' cars.

I was reminded of Herbrand Russell, the 11th Duke, and his original reason for having two cars—a brown one for the country and a black one for London. He did not like to separate man and wife overnight; consequently the brown-car chauffeur would meet the black-car chauffeur in Hendon and the 11th Duke would switch from country car to town car whenever he went to London.

That must be one of the big differences since the 11th Duke's time—now just about anyone on a salary could afford a black car and a brown car, though very few could afford a driver, let alone two drivers. In the days of the 11th Duke, Woburn had sixty to seventy indoor staff; they were now down to fewer than ten. When

I entered the house, I got the impression that most of the living happened in one familiar area, with everywhere else unlit and rarely visited.

In the car park, as I waited for Lord Howland to arrive, a security-guard type came over and didn't exactly grill me but took my name, that kind of thing. Couldn't he tell I was a gent, friend of the lord? Obviously not. Just doing his job.

Lord H appeared in his Audi Quattro. He gave the security guard curt instructions, overriding some lame chat the man came out with. That's the boss speaking, I thought. But still, imagine having to be masterful like that on a Sunday, or when you're not feeling very well. It's not that easy being a lord, I could see.

Part of Lord H's time was spent running the various enterprises that spring forth from Woburn Abbey and the estate, and part of it was spent buying and selling horses. I got the impression that the horse trading appealed to him more than estate management. But he wasn't about to give up the estate. For the whole family, ever since the safari park was set up, survival of the ancestral seat has been paramount. Lord H carries on this tradition, inspired partly by the knowledge, which he never expresses, that nothing that could replace the Bedford dynasty would be any better for the people and land of Woburn. Imagine a company with anonymous directors running the safari park. Imagine the housing developments that would be sneaked through if the estate were broken up and sold to developers. After only half an hour inside the lordly environs of Woburn Abbey, I was a fervent forelock-tugging aristocrophile.

The first and strongest reason for this was the sheer beauty of Woburn. The ancient planted trees have a huge grandeur. The manicured parkland and even beauty of the grassland, with all the herds of different deer walking about (there are red deer, Manchurian sika, Rusa, axis, fallow, muntjac, Chinese water deer, and barasingh as well as Pere Davids), give the place the feel of Eden.

The following morning I awoke early and heard the clicking of hooves outside my window. The sun was heliograph bright as it broke the horizon, laying long dawn shadows from the big Pere David stags gathered there, tails flicking. As the sun climbed higher, it lit up the orange of their early summer coats. Eden.

HOTEL

M Y ROOM in Woburn Abbey was hotel-like in its accessories: free toothbrush and lots of towels. I wondered whether hotels copied country houses, or country houses copied hotels. The room was full of old furniture and paintings that were worth looking at, with cracked glaze and skillful brushwork, a room fit for a human being, though I remember the central heating was devilishly hot.

Breakfast was in the comfortable, semimodernized part of the big house, the part where most of the living went on. The staff appeared and disappeared into dark hallways. I met a range of servants from the head of the estate to the butler and the maid. They were polite and helpful, but I wasn't imperious enough, or at ease enough, to be the perfect guest. Lord H's father was at breakfast and he was unaffectedly kind and polite. When he heard how the deer had been shot the day before, he was upset and did not hide his feelings, though his wife reminded him that it had to be done.

Outside the abbey, Tiger Moth biplanes took off and landed. They were part of a local festival. Lord H's great-great-grandmother, known as the Flying Duchess, flew a Tiger Moth; she made her first flight from Croydon to Woburn in 1928 at the age of sixty-one and gained several long-distance flying records before her death, aged seventy-two, in 1937.

I spent the morning in the estate office going through the old deer record books. It felt good to be doing real history again, connecting to the people who had saved Milu from extinction, reading their difficult handwriting.

DUKE

I N SOME circles, the 11th Duke is a villain. He is widely believed to have introduced the gray squirrel to England. He did import some to Woburn in 1894, but gray squirrels had been released in Macclesfield in 1876, and the spread of the gray squirrel did not start until its introduction into English town parks. The squirrels were an attraction for urban Victorians, who missed the comfortable sight of wild animals. Guilt, in this case, lies with every town council in England for deciding to release the aggressive American tree rodent. Even his responsibility for the muntjac invasion is now being questioned, since Whipsnade and Tring Park also released this deer into the English countryside.

But if he wasn't a bad guy, the 11th Duke was certainly eccentric, that English variety of eccentric who considers himself completely normal. While he ate breakfast, he fed his pet owl at the table because it made sense to use that time efficiently. Besides, he liked the company of owls. Intelligent birds.

He believed that the eland antelope would be a useful low-cost addition to the sheep and cows grazing the English countryside. Accordingly he had several bull calves castrated and reared for the table. This excursion into the exotic-meat market foundered when the tasting panel of his friends concluded that fresh eland had "neither the specific merits of venison nor the succulence of beef."

For health purposes, Russell liked to eat fried deer velvet taken from the antlers of culled stags. It made a tasty addition to breakfast. Full of nutrients.

Born in 1858, Russell was educated at home and then at Balliol College, Oxford. Not having suffered the conformist pressures of a public school, Russell's individuality reached its full potential, one feels.

In 1879 he joined the Grenadier Guards and fought in the 1882 Egyptian campaign. He was a brave man. At Tel-el-Kebir he was the last officer to carry regimental colors into battle, for which he received the Medal with Clasp and Khedive Star.

He long held the view that the main threat to world peace came from the Prussians, "an arrogant and truculent race of men."

In 1893 he assumed the title 11th Duke of Bedford from his brother, the 10th Duke. His civilian duties were extensive and he took them seriously. He was, among other things, president of the Zoological Society, mayor of Holborn, and president of the Cremation Society.

He was not a financial wizard. In 1895 his estates were running a joint loss of seven thousand pounds per annum. In 1914, on professional advice, he invested a hundred thousand pounds in Moscow City bonds, worth nothing three years later. He also sold Covent Garden market, the Royal Opera House, Drury Lane, the Strand, and Aldwych theaters, the Waldorf Hotel, and Bow Street Police Court: in all, nineteen acres of London's top real estate. Unfortunately, he sold them at a loss when the market was in recession. Had he kept those nineteen acres, there might have been no need to turn Woburn into the highly commercial venture it is today.

Unlike many aristocrats desperate to reverse the shift from country to urban wealth, Russell never sold the family library. The Spencers did just that in 1892, selling forty thousand volumes for £210,000. It was rumored to be the finest private library in the world, but was now no longer thought worth keeping. The sale of artworks and books by aristocrats is always a sign of decline.

CANOE

I N THE later part of the nineteenth century, the Rob Roy canoe became a symbol of healthy living and self-reliant muscular Christianity. Herbrand Russell and his wife, the Duchess Mary Russell, were both keen paddlers, spending part of each year afloat on the Tamar in Cornwall.

The Rob Roy was a one- or two-man canoe, built out of cedar on oak frames and popularized by the boxer, patent lawyer, amateur soldier, and preacher John MacGregor. Mac-Gregor saw the canoe as a metaphor for the evangelizing spirit of Christianity—it could get anywhere without running aground, on account of its needing only three inches of water to float in.

MacGregor's talks about his canoe exploits made thousands of pounds—all of which he donated to working boys' clubs. His book *A Thousand Miles in a Rob Roy Canoe* was a Victorian bestseller. MacGregor formed the Canoe Club, "for business and bivouac, for paddling and sailing, and for racing and chasing in canoes over land and water." Herbrand Russell was a hearty supporter.

Russell naturally sympathized with MacGregor's hardy brand of English Christianity, his distaste for popery, his concern for the ordinary working man, and of course his love of canoeing. Canoeing enabled one to explore on one's own, without having to give orders, without being bothered by others. Both Russell and his wife preferred action to words. Both were taciturn to an unusual degree, preferring the natural solitude of the canoe to the forced banter of the drawingroom. Years later, when the duchess took up flying solo in a Tiger Moth, she would feel that same sense of exultant solitude, above and connected to the world but never overwhelmed by it.

In Russell's Rob Roy were all the boy-scout accessories necessary for enjoyable canoeing: An odd-shaped spoon-fork, fork prongs at one end, tablespoon at the other, which tapered ingeniously to a point—this was to allow both the cracking and eating of a soft-boiled egg. The cooker was a brass primus stove of minute proportions, and the medicine chest was a matchbox containing sticking plaster and a little quinine.

We can imagine him alone, or perhaps paddling silently with Lady Russell, contemplating his various pastimes and enterprises, his duties and his plans. The blades of the paddles dipping into the wide, smooth river, he must have considered the fortunes of all his animals. It was 1900. From what Salisbury had said, China was suddenly more of a concern than Russia. There would be no more deer from there.

That he thought this through is extraordinary in itself, since no one else was doing anything remotely like it. Men had been mounting, stuffing, and classifying beasts for centuries, since Greek times. No one had thought to preserve them except as food. To preserve them from possible extinction was revolutionary.

It is all the more extraordinary because the Duke of Bedford was known to be an old-fashioned man. He preferred to wear stockings and long coats rather than the more modern suit with a jacket. He deplored noisy modern machines and only agreed to use cars because of the convenience it afforded others. He hated airplanes, and when his wife took up flying at sixty-one, he tolerated it but did not condone or even understand it.

For the first time in human history, the fogey, the old-fashioned, the regressive, and the reactionary was actually at the forefront of important developments.

The terrific slaughter of the American bison was a working model for Russell. It was a highly visible demonstration of what happened when modern hunting techniques were applied with scientific care. Nostalgia for the old Wild West led for calls to save the bison. The methods were rudimentary—simply allow the bison to roam in parks where they would not be hunted.

Bison conservation had been a homegrown American operation. Russell's idea of genius was to apply this model to saving any species from any country. Concern for foreign animals was a bit like concern for foreign nationals—an unusual eccentricity. But Russell's eccentricity was Milu's saving.

Not only was the idea a new one, but it depended on such technological innovations as the Suez Canal, which shortened the journey home from China, and steamboats and railways, which allowed the animals to be distributed to zoos and circuses in Europe. Without this rapid, large-scale distribution system, any attempt at saving a species as far away from home as Milu would have been inconceivable.

Technology had caused the breakup of China and, indirectly,

the extinction of Milu in its own country. But paradoxically, technology had allowed Milu to survive.

Like many original ideas, the saving of Milu crept up on Herbrand Russell. It wasn't the product of just one meditative holiday afloat on the Tamar River. One can imagine the cumulative thinking of several summers, paddling around, slowly arriving at the grand idea.

RUSSELL, EARLIER

As an undergraduate at Balliol College, Oxford, Russell was drawn into a group of high-spirited sportsmen. Wagers and challenges were their only interest. On one occasion he was given the choice between chopping down Benjamin Jowett's favorite tree—a three-hundred-year-old mulberry tree—or poaching a deer from the park in nearby Magdalen College.

The leader of these ruffians was one A. J. H. Hartley, a tall, gangling fellow with a penchant for shooting at policemen with a rook rifle. The deer would have to be hanging in the meat larder of Hartley's servant in Hythe Bridge Street by dawn of the appointed day. If not, the forfeit could only be delayed by chopping down the tree and leaving it as faggots on the doorstep of Jowett's lodgings. This too before the renowned Master of Balliol awoke and took his morning bowl of meat broth.

Failing both challenges, the forfeit was one hundred pounds,

170

to be placed in the cap of the first beggar encountered that day in the low district of Jericho. Success would bring only honor and the chance to accept future challenges.

Their plan was simple enough. Affix the nets, which were extensive, between two trees in the dark end of the deer park. Then approach a sleeping or grazing deer with stealth and drive it toward the net. It was poaching with no finesse.

They had agreed upon a young male, but quickly saw that it would be a case of snaring whatever they could. Russell didn't like that side of it, but then it was a rag and to be expected.

The deer shifted uneasily across the grass as the young men approached. Lloyd-Evans, Russell's second, indicated a nervous doe that dipped its head to eat and then looked up every few seconds. The nets were in place. This was their chance. They started in at a silent walk, intent on the prey. The doe lifted its head again. They stopped. Lloyd-Evans nodded very slightly. Both men started to run. The doe and half a dozen other deer fled with effortless speed over the hard turf. Both men were sprinting as fast as they had ever run and were still lagging behind. But it was the finest feeling to be running on foot after deer. Russell had hunted on horseback and stalked on the estate in Scotland, but this running was the finest feeling.

With a dull thwack the doe hit the loosely hung net. Its head and foreleg were trapped for a minute. Long enough for the young men to be on it with their simple weapons. Now the deer was barking, a pathetic low-toned bleat of fear, which nevertheless sounded as loud as Great Tom striking to Russell and Lloyd-Evans.

Lloyd-Evans used his nobby black wood club, again and again

at the side of the skull. "No different to taking a priest to a perch's head," he said, breathing hard. Russell used the net to entrap the deer further and hold it still.

Russell was no sentimentalist. He had shot deer, rabbits, pigeons, grouse, pheasants, and partridge. He had clubbed fish to death on a riverbank. He'd seen a fox's head ripped half away by two hounds. But this clubbing of the roe deer was different. The elemental brutality of it. The fact that it wouldn't die easily. This was the way savages behaved.

In the end Lloyd-Evans stabbed it six times in the back of the neck with the stiletto he carried everywhere. "Hartley would be proud of you," said a grim Russell.

Rolling the limp beast in the net, they carried it like a heavy sack toward the wall of the park. Humping it to the top of the wall, Russell suddenly motioned for silence. A bobbing lamp was coming along the perimeter toward them. Coming at a jogging pace. They could only crouch on the wall and wait. Russell sensed Lloyd-Evans adjust the grip on his club. The proctor came toward them, not looking up, half walking fast, half hurrying his steps into a run; preoccupied with his breathing, he didn't see two men and a deer in the bright moonlight above him.

"Do you know," said Lloyd-Evans, as they swaggered home, having stowed the beast with Hartley's tame servant, "I would have knocked that man down if he'd tried to stop us."

"And I might have helped you," said Russell. He never hunted again.

* * *

For some reason this proved to be the last real challenge proposed by the raffish Hartley and his friends. Months later, Herbrand Russell came down from Oxford and took a commission in the Grenadier Guards.

The mulberry tree still stands in the Balliol Fellow's Garden.

EDEN

THE PLACE where it all started, the place where all species are represented in full, before depletion by time, meteor attack, or the work of the Major and his friends. Eden stands at the opposite end of the spectrum to the dead world, the world extinguished of all life, what scientists gleefully tell us we have to look forward to in 150 million years.

But the phrase "look forward to" only has meaning with regard to events that can be looked forward to, that are within a sensible human time frame—within my lifetime, or my children's, say. It is utterly meaningless to draw any ordinary conclusions from the supposed knowledge that the world will be extinguished long in the future. It's just an easily told story, nothing more. The opposite of Eden, the smoking, charred corpse of a planet that Earth is destined to become, is, in any meaningful sense, an invention of the science-fiction writer's mind.

CHERNOBYL

SURPRISING FOOTAGE from Chernobyl, filmed from radio-controlled planes fitted with video cameras—the place is teeming with wildlife. In the absence of man, animals return even to the poisoned zones. Deer, rabbits, foxes, field mice—all running through the deserted concrete shells of towns, past the abandoned cars and open doorways and the trees growing up through cracks in the road.

EDEN II

CONSERVATION IS an attempt to fix Eden, but in life things keep on developing. That which looks fixed is an optical illusion.

The moment conservation becomes thinkable, Eden slips from our grasp, since wild animals are no longer wild if they can be conserved, corralled, looked after. They are tame animals in danger. Wild plants and animals do exist, but they are hardly exotic—rodents, feral pigeons, certain snakes, undersoil fungi, woodlice, cockroaches. Animals that often accompany man in his dwelling places but are not controlled by man. Survivors.

Eden after the fall is defined by these survivors: its pests and parasites, its weeds and scavengers, its unwanted population and its mountains of garbage.

Just as a petri dish full of multiplying bacteria will eventually poison itself with its own excreta, so the human race races up to the limit of self-poisoning before maintaining an uneasy symbiosis with its waste products. The animals closest to us now are the ones that eat our prodigious filth. Our friends the rats, the roaches, the seagulls on the landfill outside town.

MISTAKE

I HADN'T HEARD from the Major for months so I decided to send him a postcard. I sent one of Woburn Abbey. Even though he would never admit it, I knew that a postcard would be welcome. I was careful to keep the message bland: no mention of Milu or even my connection to Woburn. I avoided, too, any words that might annoy the man, words like *conservation, ecology,* or even *nature.* Europe's first nature reserves, he was found of pointing out, had been built in Hitler's Germany. To the Major, all greenies were crypto-Nazis.

HISTORY

ROM THE deer records I could see that for the first few months of a deer's life it was hard to tell if it was male or female—there was a special column in the record book for "sex indeterminate." After a month or two, sex indeterminates graduated into either males or females. I wondered what I would think if I came across this book a few centuries from now, perhaps with no other supporting documents. I might think that those fools in the past actually believed that deer went through an asexual phase before becoming either male or female. I might assume that, on the written evidence I had in front of me, if I knew nothing of deerkeeping. Fortunately, Callum had told me earlier, "It's bloody hard to tell if a calf is male or female, not without bringing them in for a thorough examination, and we're not going to do that."

WORLD WAR I

THE DRIVER knew better than to speed through the estate. His master, the duke, now colonel-commanding, sat in the back, working through papers that related to war and the management of men to fight that war. He took in the numbers, the numbers of men they would need to recruit. The "target" figures set by the War Office. Already half the estate was fighting; they were down to a skeleton staff working halfway into the night. The papers spoke of "the spirit and self-sacrifice of the New Armies." How "if they had been able to devote more time to training they would have been able to hold on to many points of importance, but from which they were driven by the enterprising German machine-gunners."

Russell had fought in Egypt; he knew war and thought it no more or less than man's estate, in these troubled times, the Prussian tribe grown noisy and seeking dominion and the English soul clamoring for a chance to wield the sword. He had known war, yet this war was proving different. A shake of the head wouldn't make that difference go away. Finding no pleasure in duty, commerce with the public, acts of office, vainpuffery, and manorial license, the duke nevertheless did everything that was required of him. At the tail end of a world where public office meant power and the freedom to be mightily eccentric, the duke pursued his daily round of duties with an actor's forbearance, an actor who can rarely leave the stage.

Herbrand Russell looked up, saw the trees black against the dark-blue evening sky. Some way ahead there were lights in the village and, carrying faintly, the rising and falling sound of a church bell. He stowed his papers in a scratched leather briefcase. Dimmed the acetylene reading lamp. He had always followed the rules, done what he wanted, but within the rules. Now the rules were taking on an insidious life of their own. Cattle and sheep were arriving daily, a "quota" that the estate "must support." He had received the official documents from the estate office, crude calculations made from erroneous figures purporting to show the number of beasts the estate should farm; domesticated beasts— the deer didn't count anymore. The real work of his life could very well be slaughtered by a clerk making a calculation about sheep and cattle. Very little hay had been grown, and the winter grass was pitifully overgrazed. The sheep would go to market, but more would take their place. The Pere David's deer would die, the meat disappearing into grateful stews and game pies from Woburn Sands to Ampthill, and Milu would be no more.

No *damnum fatale.* This must not be allowed to happen. Wearing a stern face close to the glass of the side window, the car gathering pace over the iron cattle-grid, he felt no self-pity but a determination to hug the burden of his life closer, what he had made himself, without the rules. He glimpsed some great catastrophe on the horizon. Moving through lifetimes and coming to meet men soon.

FARM SAVE

My mother telephoned. She hadn't won the lottery, but she had been to visit the old farm all the same. She had gone with my aunt. My aunt had said, "When you leave the home you were brought up in, you always feel a bit homeless all your life." They were torn between sadness at seeing the old place, what with all the caravans and it being not as neat as my grandfather kept it, and that curious nosy pleasure of poking around in an updated version of the past. My mother said that the people they talked to who hadn't moved away had a much better memory of the old days than she or my aunt did.

When the auction occurred, the farm didn't reach its reserve price. There was still a chance we might be able to buy it back in the future.

EGYPT VII

PEOPLE SAID *I ought to meet Lothar if I was so interested in books. Lothar had a huge number of books and he'd certainly know where to get more. Lothar was also the official German biographer of Nobel prizewinner Naguib Mahfouz. Anyone who wanted to meet Mahfouz had to meet Lothar first.*

In 1992 Naguib Mahfouz had been stabbed in the neck by two Islamic fundamentalist students. This attempted assassination was prompted by Mahfouz's book Children of Gebelaawi, *which he'd written thirty years earlier. The book was considered to have atheistic leanings and was banned in Egypt, though Nadim said he knew a shop where we could get it under the counter. Since the stabbing, Mahfouz had been weakened. He was often too weak to write. He no longer went to the coffee shops in Khan al Kalil.*

Lothar had translated many of Mahfouz's works into German, though not Children of Gebelaawi. *It was the translation connection that led to Mahfouz agreeing that he could be his official German biographer.*

It turned out that I had been in the same room as Lothar on a previous visit to Cairo, though I did not remember him. The mutual friend whose room Lothar and I had been in put us in touch. Lothar invited us to an Iftar supper at his Nile-side apartment on Zamalek, just past the 23 July Bridge, a very classy location. In fact, I couldn't resist asking him the cost of his apartment. It was rent controlled, less than two hundred U.S. dollars a month, with big, high-ceilinged rooms, double doors, and a balcony big enough for a party. Lothar had invited some people over to meet my wife and me, which was very civil of him.

Lothar's houseboy tended to the two large charcoal braziers that glowed on the balcony in massive upturned woklike contraptions. The boy then scuttled in and finished off the cooking. Lothar said that he had taught him how to cook himself.

I'd already see Lothar's book collection—pristine, along one side of the large, dark living room, it reached from floor to ceiling. Although everyone had said Lothar had lots of books, there did not seem so many to me. But they were nicely laid out.

All the big books were on a shelf that just fitted their size. The same was true of the small-format books. Lothar said, "I got the shelving made to fit the books. Now when I buy a new book I have to throw one away the same size."

I thought he was joking, but this is in fact exactly what he did. He had decided that one thousand books was enough for anyone. When he decided to buy a new book—and it was a tough thing to decide, he intimated—he would then chuck one away.

I noticed that all the books looked new. This was because Lothar never bought secondhand books. When I quizzed him about Ezbekiya Gardens, he said he'd heard about it but that he had never been there. He told me he had a rota system for dusting his books—one shelf was dusted every month. No one else was allowed to do it except Lothar. His previous houseboy had been fired for touching his books. "They don't respect them," he said.

By now I could hardly bring myself to ask Lothar to lend me some books to read. As a way of sidling up, I said half-jocularly, "Have you earmarked any books to throw away?" "No," he said. That was it. All I could do was gaze at the pristine ranks of books in their dust jackets, admittedly a lot of German and Arabic titles but a pretty good showing of English books too, including obscure books of literary criticism, which I find always make good holiday reading.

Outside, by the glowing charcoal braziers, Lothar spoke about Naguib Mahfouz. People asked him respectful questions about the Nobel prizewinner's health, current opinions, whether he would publish again. Lothar gave considered replies to all such questions. It was not hard to see that he relished being the gatekeeper. He then spoke about all the famous people he had met who had wanted to meet Naguib Mahfouz—they'd needed him not just as a contact but also as a translator.

"What's Naguib Mahfouz like?" I said.

Lothar looked at me quickly. "He always says 'we' when he means 'I.' It's a kind of courtesy peculiar to his generation."

As we were leaving, I overheard Lothar explaining that his book would take many more years to complete. "It's exhaustive," he said. "The last word." I understood then that Naguib Mahfouz was his scam, like the pyramids and the mega-expensive bookshop, there to attract people in. If he finished the biography, the scam would have to end.

I'm in the Dark

THE NOVELIST'S latest novel was at proof stage. He was now checking for typos and small errors. Auk Books were generous; unlike some publishers, they didn't charge the author if the number of typos went above two hundred. This novel, the breakthrough novel, was about the dark. Most of the novel took place in a house where the lights were never switched on and the curtains were always drawn and it was always night and the occupants were blind anyway. Always wearing dark glasses. The prose was dazzling, like cut glass, Klaudia said. The prose was the only thing that wasn't completely dark. Or it was dark, but like black cut glass it flashed light darkly.

"Your next novel," I said to the Novelist. "It sounds dark."

"Yep," he said. "In fact, Klaudia suggested we call it *The Dark.* What do you think?"

"Perfect title."

I'm not trying to belittle the Novelist. His novel had lots of other good things in it. A subplot involving a World War II commando raid on Norway. A singing automaton that also played chess. A pair of Siamese twins who hated each other's guts even though they had the same guts. Breakthrough stuff if handled in the right way, and I believed wholeheartedly that if anyone could handle such material it would be the Novelist. Just sitting and drinking beer with him (his favorite was real ale brewed in Southwold), one's confidence in him grew and grew. You felt you were on some trawler out in the North Sea, with his capable hands on the wheel. A storm of words was brewing up, but he was rock solid. By the fourth pint it was hard to understand why he hadn't already won a Nobel Prize.

In fact, talking about Nobel Prizes, the Novelist is the only person I've ever met who not only knows 1951 Nobel winner Pär Lagerkvist's name but has actually read his novel *Det Besegrade Livet (Triumph Over Lies).* In Norwegian.

The Novelist also liked to talk about T. S. Eliot. He contended that the original *Waste Land* (before Ezra Pound edited it) was all about light and how that symbolized for Eliot the vital source of all life, the creative life force, if you like. And more than being just a symbol, it was something Eliot had really experienced. Only when he wrote about it, well, it was just a bit too much, a bit over the top. Pound stripped it right out and turned *The Waste Land* into a nostalgia piece, a fashionably fagged-out shoring-fragments-against-the-ruins piece. This interested the Novelist because (a) he considered the Pound version better literature than anything Eliot wrote unaided and (b) he wondered if there is now, of all times, a basic hostility between literature and truth. The Novelist told me that people had been suspicious of literature before, that in medieval Arabic there was no word, as we now use it, for *literature*. My wife confirmed this.

But what I really wanted to know was what his next novel would be about, the one after the breakthrough novel. But though I pried and hinted and spied, he would never tell me.

CON AIR

I ASKED LORD H if I might help Callum with the annual deer cull. If he thought it was a macabre request, he politely kept his opinion to himself and asked Callum to take me along for the week when the main cull took place. Now I was where I wanted to be, albeit in a paradoxical position. I was writing a book about an endangered species, and here I was rubbing my hands together at the prospect of dispatching them from the planet. The Major would definitely have approved.

Scroll back a bit, to the previous summer. I had, for some unfathomable reason, become obsessed with hunting. I had tried to gain a firearms certificate, but that required a letter from your GP to say that you weren't insane. The certificate also required references from landowners. It also hinted that every time someone was shot, the police would be around for a fireside chat and a sniff at your gun barrel (which had to be in a locked steel cabinet or else). All this just to kill innocent creatures. My friend Mark, a forester, who had the chance to shoot but chose not to, said, "A gun in this country, it's like being a bit overdressed, isn't it?"

The obsession waned. The only GP I knew was already a hate figure because of the offhand way she'd treated my wife just after our son was born. In fact, we had had such a rough experience with the medical establishment that I couldn't bear to bring myself to ask them if I was sane or not.

Now that I had the chance to pop off at some harmless Pere Davids, my old hunting urges returned. I secretly hoped Callum would let me "take down" a couple, or even just one. Maybe he'd let me keep the antlers as a memento. I wouldn't ask, though; well, not until I knew him pretty well.

I excitedly told Klaudia that I was finally going to get near to some deer-slaying action, hoping that this would make her feel I wasn't being slack about the book. I told her my wife had had a baby, and she asked the usual polite questions about health, sleeping habits, etc.

I'd told everyone that suddenly becoming a father wasn't going to interfere with my traveling. And here I was proving it—going off to Woburn and leaving my wife to her own devices just a few weeks after the child had been born.

This time I wasn't staying in the main house. I would be in Lord H's pad, a ranch-style bungalow with a swimming pool on the edge of the estate. Actually I was going to be in the guest wing and Lord H would be in the main part of the bungalow. Then I heard that Lord H was staying on for a day or two in Scotland, so the first night I was put up at his expense at the pretty expensive Bedford Arms Hotel.

That night I sat in the bar and watched. *Con Air* on the television. Normally I hate TVs in bars, but tonight, being alone, I was pleased it was there. A middle-aged/elderly man made comments at regular intervals to the bartender about how bad it was to have a television on in a bar. Fortunately for me, the bartender did not have the authority to turn the TV off. Maybe only the manager could make important decisions like that.

In the end, the company of the bartender and the grumpy old-ish man was spoiling my enjoyment of the film. They had got together now and were deep in the sort of conversation that seemed designed to show that though both of them actually had a natural antipathy toward each other, they could "talk to anyone."

A man from Liverpool came in and asked if there was anywhere in town to get a bite. I'd already had some food at a pub up the road and told him so. This was my entire conversation for the evening, which would have been pretty depressing if *Con Air* hadn't been on.

I retired to my room for the final part of the film. Of course, this was something of a letdown. For some reason the plot ended with a big one-location showdown in the desert with lots of crashing planes and jeeps and tanks and with the police just arriving over the hill. The filmmakers had made a mistake. They should have kept the film moving, like *North by Northwest*. Since *Con Air* was about bugger all, it should at least have been dynamic. Instead of a literal grounding-out there should have been a sequence of air sequences, each smaller than the last: jumbo jet, Learjet, turbo prop, helicopter, biplane, microlight, hang glider, parachute. The film was aptly titled because it *was* a con air, since half of it took place on the ground.

It was pretty stupid staying up late watching the film, because the cull was due to start the next day at 5:30 A.M. outside the estate office.

I booked an alarm call with reception to be on the safe side. I knew that Callum wouldn't hang around if I were late, and, of course, I felt constrained to appear at least vaguely professional.

EXPERTS

EARLIER, WHEN I had arrived, Callum had taken me up to where there were some pedigree red deer to feed. I had carried a bucket of feed just to show myself willing, but I could tell that Callum didn't really need me to muck in. They weren't short staffed, and they too wanted to look professional, i.e., not requiring help from passing writers.

I hate being on the receiving end of "professionalism." You

feel excluded and bored. And trying to be "professional" usually means copying a procedure or relying on a machine. Both of these are signs of lack of faith in one's own human abilities.

The problem is that people have to protect themselves. My friend Mark, the forester, claims he needs lots of expensive machines, otherwise potential "clients" won't think he's "professional," even though he assures me he isn't in favor of all the machines he has. The machines and systems and paperwork become something to hide behind, a kind of necessary fakery everyone requires. It is as if we have convinced ourselves that life really is very complicated and therefore to be taken seriously. If things were too simple, we might think life was too easy. So we make life complicated and the pain of trying to figure things out both takes up time and seems worrying and by extension serious. There seems to be this complication threshold; if we can manage to dip below it we start actually thinking about our lives—I mean our real lives, not our outer career lives.

CULLS

CALLUM'S LIGHTS came slowly closer as he drove toward where I was parked in front of the estate office. He was a bit grim-faced when I got into his Land Rover. "Every year I look forward to this less and less," he told me. "It's not like stalking."

We drove at less than walking pace across the darkened park-land. A few hundred yards away was the assistant keeper in his Hi-Lux. We coordinated our moves with his over the hand-held radio. Callum knew the position the main herd would be in at dawn. We parked under huge oak trees and waited for first light. I'd already had an early morning cigarette, but if I hadn't this would have been the time to smoke one. "Can deer smell smoke?" I started to ask Callum, but at that moment he grabbed the radio and told the assistant we were going in. He put the radio down and then remembered I'd spoken. "What?" he asked. "Nothing," I said. We were going in.

The herd stood grazing, over two hundred of them spread out in front of us with a slight mist lying in the hollows, making them look like wraiths. It was a curious experience, because as a child I had for a while believed that ghosts appeared in the form of elk or large deer—it was only later, aged seven or so, that I learned that ghosts were dead humans come back to haunt us.

Culling is more difficult than ordinary deer-shooting. You might think that having the pick of a big, relatively tame herd would be easy, but it isn't. The first consideration is background. "We don't want to shoot anyone down in the town," said Callum. If the shot wasn't against a slight rise in the land, a miss could go for another two miles and still be lethal. Next was the problem of deer standing in front of each other—again, a miss, or a bullet leaving one beast and entering another, could cause unwanted injury or death. Finally, when you had an isolated deer in your sights against a slight incline, you had to be sure it was one of those intended for the cull. Today we were after "spikers," young males of around eighteen months.

To outsiders the idea of culling an endangered species must seem mad. Pere Davids are among the rarest deer in the world, and we were just about to blow a few away before breakfast.

Some people who have received Pere Davids from Woburn refuse to cull. Often these deer reduce their surroundings to bare ground and barkless trees. They escape and interbreed with red deer, or are shot on other people's land. Or they so crowd the limited environment they are kept in that disease takes its toll. Now that Pere Davids all live in controlled environments, they need to be culled.

At this point, though deer aren't really at all like humans, I was beginning to identify with them strongly. I allowed my mind to explore the idea of human culling. After all, we all live in controlled environments now. Overpopulation is imminent everywhere. In some countries there is not enough food, in others not enough land or natural resources. Countries that have imposed strict birth control, like China, have ended up with skewed populations of more boys than girls, because girls are often aborted after a scan. Everywhere people complain about how there isn't enough land anymore, how the world is being used up too quickly.

The simple answer, I darkly fantasized, would be a human cull. Teams of trained marksmen would go out and search for herds of humans—probably young males and females, the human equivalent of spikers. Once they'd staked out a herd, say a queue for a nightclub or a football match, they could wait for a clear shot against a safe background. Couples leaving late at night might be safest to pick off, especially with infrared night vision.

"Do you ever use night-vision equipment?" I asked Callum.

"We looked into it," he said. "But too many weirdos walk through the park at night. We might have ended up killing someone we couldn't properly see. At least in daylight you can judge the background properly."

Maybe the human cull would have to be a daylight job too. It would be a terrible job to do—very stressful. The cullers would have to be men of the highest moral fiber. Imagine if parents bribed them not to cull their offspring? Disaster. Culling would have to be seen to be fair.

The first few culls would have to be very heavy, to make any dent in the population at all. There would have to be a whole subsidiary industry to get rid of the bodies.

My fantasizing ground to a halt when I started to invent reasons why I alone should not be culled. . . .

Dark thoughts for a dark night, but dawn was almost upon us.

Callum wound down his window and sighted his rifle on an isolated spiker at the far right side of the herd, resting the gun on the big wing mirror. Without warning he flipped on a pair of plastic earmuffs. Shit, I thought, and immediately jammed my fingers in my ears. I'd been caught out before by being close to gunfire— the noise, especially in an enclosed space, is the most shocking thing about it. I'm surprised more old soldiers aren't completely deaf.

There was, after a long wait, the huge expected bang and the deer fell hard, straight to the ground. A head shot. Callum preferred head shots to the more usual heart shot because the animal died instantly and didn't upset the others too much. A heart shot could also result in considerable internal damage to other organs, lowering the sale price of the carcass. All culled Pere Davids are sold as top-class venison.

The next shot Callum took he missed. "Shit," he said. I could tell he didn't like missing. Then the assistant missed a shot so they were even. And two Pere Davids lived for another day.

After each beast was slain it was humped by the antlers onto the low-loader trailer, which was soon awash with blood. We—well, they—shot five deer, which was enough for one day, said Callum. He took great care to cover up the animals with a green tarpaulin. "I like to keep as low a profile as possible," he explained. "Shoot before people get up, and deliver the deer to be dressed without anyone being disturbed by the sight of them." Anyone who saw our convoy crossing the main road of the estate might think we had a trailer of feed or some other innocuous cargo, "And that's the way I like to keep it," said Callum.

There was something of the undertaker in his concern for decorum, for people's feelings about seeing dead creatures. Partly, no doubt, it was common sense. There were enough fools prating about cruelty to animals without supplying them with further ammunition. Yet wasn't there also a feeling of shame, that what we were doing wasn't quite right?

We were killing innocent animals. We were daring to threaten the levels of the animal population.

But though nobody wants to do it, killing has to be done.

That is why we had to hide the carcasses under a green tarpaulin.

DRESSING DOWN

At the deer larder I was in for a shock. The place was high-roofed but not large, two rooms, one with an overhead rail on which to hang the dead meat, the other full of black plastic bins ready for deer feet and offal.

Callum set to with a knife and a hacksaw, slicing through ligaments and sawing through bones to remove the hooves and inner organs. He wore a white overall and worked almost indecently fast. I was in the way, but had to watch. This was butchery at its finest, British hard work at its most efficient and quick. "We like to get a momentum going," said Callum. "Get the job done quickly." I could see that mucking about with blood and entrails when you hadn't even eaten breakfast was not something to linger over. After the fifth deer had been dressed I was ready to leave. The bins were humped onto the trailer, again covered, and driven off to be disposed of as food for wild animals in the safari park. No one could say they didn't get fresh meat.

PAD

I CHECKED OUT of the hotel and into Lord H's personal pad, the luxury bungalow with the indoor swimming pool. I was in the guest wing of the pad. The housekeeper was very friendly, but I realized quickly that it was a self-catering setup. I had corrections to make to a book I was writing, but something was wrong about this place. I decided the windows were too low. My feet could be seen from outside, if there had been anyone outside, and this made the place feel cold and distracting. I needed, I told myself, cozy places to write, places where my lower body couldn't be seen from outside. I switched on the television instead of working.

The housekeeper came over and told me that Lord H had left a message. He had been further detained in Scotland and wouldn't now be back until Thursday.

I drove out to a local town that evening to get fish and chips and a nice bottle of wine. Back in the guest wing with the too-low windows, I drank my wine and wondered if I was missing the noise and disrupted nights provided by my new son.

The next day my alarm went off, but allowing myself a few minutes' lie-in, I realized I'd missed the start of that day's cull. Seen one, seen them all, I said, and persuaded myself I'd go down to the deer larder at seven-thirty.

At nine o'clock I met Callum by the side of the road. He smiled wryly when I made my excuses and then turned the subject to a detective problem. Someone had reported seeing a dead deer on the road. Callum had his dog, an expensive Bavarian Mountain Hound, sniffing around for clues. We found blood, but no deer. Then the man who had reported it clarified that he had actually seen only a leg of a deer. "It must have fallen from a bin," said Callum, "as we drove over the road."

After this I spent some time watching the Pere Davids just grazing. I sat in my car alternately sipping coffee from a polystyrene cup, smoking, and looking at the deer through Callum's excellent Zeiss binoculars.

But there is a limit to how much deer-watching you can do, even of a rare and endangered species.

I thought about my wife at home with our new son. I surprised myself by how much I was missing him. Being on my own didn't seem as much fun as it usually was. Maybe some fatherhood hormone had kicked in. I thought about another evening of fish and chips (or pie and chips for a change). Another "decent" bottle of wine. The 11th Duke had been right—a man shouldn't be separated from his wife and children.

I stopped off at Callum's office for a while and chewed the fat. "This book," he said, "it must be a minority interest. It's not like your snake book. Most people aren't going to be interested in deer, are they?" I had to admire Callum's no-nonsense regard for the subject of his profession. Callum had made me welcome, but I thought he would be relieved when I had gone. As far as deer management went, I was just an obstacle to efficiency.

* * *

That evening there was another message from Lord H. He was going to be held up another few days in Scotland. I drove out to the local town where I had bought the fish and chips. This time I focused my attention on the pies. The pies inside the hot cabinet were squashed looking and wrapped in see-through plastic. I noticed the plastic seemed to be going brown on the inside. I settled for a saveloy and chips.

When I came out of the pie shop I found that the wine shop had inexplicably closed early. Saveloy and telly, or saveloy, pub, and telly? Now I was really feeling homesick.

I binned the remains of my "dinner" and drove quickly back to Woburn. I told the housekeeper I was leaving that night, left a note for Lord H on the guest-wing table, and drove off.

When I got home I was really pleased to see my son and hardly noticed that he woke us up four times that night.

CONSCIENCE

Now I'd done with Woburn it was time to think about America and China. Callum had hinted that I could go along to an exotic game hunt at Woburn later on in the year. This was when rich, usually American clients came and shot older Pere Davids at five thousand pounds a time. These were also deer that had to be culled (culling is spread right across the age groups). I thought this would be just as good as the ranch in Texas.

To square my conscience (i.e., so that I could tell Klaudia I'd tried to get a commission to go to the United States), I rang up an editor I know at *Bollux!*, a relatively new men's magazine. The editor was keen on the idea of killing things, but he wanted me to accompany Ted Nugent, the heavy-metal rock star, who's really into bow hunting.

"I think you have to shoot these deer with guns," I said.

"Do they have lions?" he asked. "Or tigers! . . . Or . . . elephants! Shoot me an elephant with tusks and it's a deal!" he shouted, hoarse with excitement.

Forget America, I told myself. The last time I went there I got the distinct impression no one gave a toss about what I was saying. New York is OK, all that energy, etc., except there can't be many Pere Davids waiting to be shot in downtown Manhattan. American men seem to have deeper voices than Brits, and even the real basket-cases talk more confidently and fluently than us. You really have to learn a whole new body language to get anywhere in the States, and there wasn't enough time to do that. . . . OK, OK, I think I've generated enough feeble excuses for not shooting yet more of the highly endangered Pere David's deer.

CHINA

NEXT ON the list was China. I bought the Lonely Planet guide to Beijing. Hmm. The thing that really caught my attention was that there was a shooting range outside town where you could shoot rocket-propelled grenades and bazookas. For some reason the rest did not seem very enticing. Lonely Planet guides often have useful stuff in them, though any town about which they say "Not worth a visit" is always worth a visit. Often the reverse is true too. The deep premise of Lonely Planet is a studenty concept of consumer tourism. Instead of consuming expensive things, LP directs people to cheap things, cheap hotels, cheap drinks.

I admit I probably sound bitter and twisted about something as innocuous as a guidebook, but to me the whole backpacking phenomenon is deeply off-putting. In my experience, most backpackers are narrow-minded, tightfisted people with suntans and Lonely Planet guidebooks. I used to be a backpacker so I know what I'm talking about. I was the original tightwad— going into carpet shops for free cups of tea, paying only for my share of the taxi, arguing over 10p on the restaurant bill. Backpacking should be illegal. All Lonely Planet guides should be burned. People should travel with Herodotus or Caesar's Gallic Wars instead.

REASONS

MY WIFE advised me to call Klaudia. I dialed her number with some trepidation. We had not spoken for a while, and after the usual remarks I gambited:

ME: Is it absolutely essential for me to go to China?
KLAUDIA: Yes. Do you have a problem with that?
ME: Er, no, not really.

What I found hard to weave into the phone conversation was a premonition I'd had that I should not go. That would have segued very nicely into a story about Robert Capa, the great war photographer, who reluctantly went to Vietnam just to earn some money to pay bills. He was through with war and he just didn't want to go. Within a short time of arriving he was dead, having stood on a mine in a paddy field.

I thought about Capa's last picture, not nearly so well known as his famous (probably faked) picture of a man being shot in the Spanish Civil War. This last picture, though, is much more haunting. It is a blurry, out-of-focus shot of a lot of sky and some trees at a crazy angle. It is the picture he took just as he stood on the mine, pressing the shutter exactly as he was being blown up.

When you don't want to go, you really shouldn't go. That's what this part of me was saying.

Turned Down

By now the world Milu expert, Maja Boyd, had shared her thoughts about the project with Lord H. He passed the letter on to me. She had read my proposal and was not pleased. After a page listing my "errors," she wrote:

> Twigger calls the Milu "freakish"—actually the Milu is the least freakish ungulate. As you know, you can approach them very close and they stand and look at you as if they were a little dumb.... True, he has read some books, but he does not distinguish reality from fiction ... if you give him permission to write his book, you need to have final rights to make changes in order to make sure that facts are accurate and, as important, that the tone of the book is "fair," as you would not like our Chinese friends to be upset whenever they read the book.

I wrote explaining why my proposal was so full of craven errors. I wrote begging for assistance. There was no reply.

EDEN'S PRICE

Now I fell into a frenzied depression. I'd been snubbed by the world's expert on Pere David's deer! And I was supposed to be writing a book about PERE DAVID'S DEER! I began to panic. Maybe I would not be able to write the book. My wife advised that I call Klaudia again. I asked her whether we had spent the first part of the advance. Maybe we could return it and forget the whole thing. Killing the deer, or watching them being killed, hadn't been such a good idea. Despite an attraction to guns and the like I was a softie, urban despite my affectations of country sensibilities. I was fed up with killing, and every time I made contact with Pere David's deer there was always some killing to be done. I wasn't prepared to pay Eden's price.

I sat at the computer and wrote MILU in big letters. Then I altered the font several times. Usually I write in Courier (i.e., normal typewriter type), but Courier needs courage. I tried Helvetica, then Times Roman; even Palatino, the most confident of fonts, failed me.

It was time to get radical.

EXTINCTION II

BUT NOW I was beginning to understand at least one small thing about extinction. Extinction does not start with starvation. Extinction does not start with illness and disease. Extinction starts with the absence of the will to go on. In the grand scheme of things my writing was not important. But it was important to me, and what kept me writing was *very* important to me. I saw my will to keep writing as a specialized minor form of the will to keep living.

Take the great auk, which became extinct about 150 years ago—unlike the Pacific snail, its extinction cannot be dated precisely. About thirty inches high, with a giant beak and black-and-white plumage, the great auk (or garefowl) was like a Northern Hemisphere version of the penguin. Although the beak of the great auk was weirder than any penguin's, more like a hornbill.

It is tempting to ascribe at least partial responsibility for the great auk's demise to its extreme oddness. If any bird was going to be picked on, the big-beaked auk is an obvious choice. One specimen was executed on Saint Kilda as a witch because it was said to have caused a terrible storm. Another was kept as a pet and allowed to swim at the end of a piece of string in the filthy waters of the River Clyde.

Unlike the dodo, the great auk inhabited a wide geographic

spread of habitats—rocks, skerries, and islands along the inhospitable northern coasts of the Atlantic. That it was hastened to its death by hunting is indubitable, but it is not quite correct to suggest that overhunting was the sole cause of its extinction.

Many birds are hunted until there are only a few breeding pairs left. Ospreys and peregrine falcons, though enjoying a healthy comeback, even breeding in London, were so persecuted by prewar gamekeepers that they all but disappeared from Britain. But the big difference between the great auk and a bird of prey is that the auk likes company, lots of company.

It shared with its fellow extinctee, the passenger pigeon, a predilection for living in large, highly visible groups. On Funk Island, off Newfoundland, the original colony numbered over ten thousand. For three hundred years it was used as a convenient source of meat and feathers by fishermen sailing that coast, and despite regular pillaging (there are still little stone compounds where great auks were kept alive until needed) the birds did not choose to go elsewhere. They were excellent swimmers. There were plenty of places to go if only the colony had decided to move.

But the great auk seemed to need a certain threshold number to survive. Colonies that dipped below a certain level did not split up, could not split up. It was as if the great auk *did not exist* when its group went below a certain high number.

Biologists have observed this in bacteria and call it quorum sensing—below a certain number, a colony of bacteria is "unintelligent," cannot cooperate in order to repel attackers. When it attains quorum numbers, intracellular communication takes place. One result is the formation of a self-protective biofilm.

The great auk is also quorum sensitive. Below a certain very high number, the population just acts dumb, waiting for the ax to fall.

This sounds silly, hard to believe. In our own age, where the fantasy of the individual is at its strongest, an unexplained need for others seems somehow weak. We forget that prehistoric man wasn't a loner. He divided up basic tasks among a viable group. In most places where man has chosen to live, life is too hard for not only one man alone but even one small family alone. At the barest functional level, people need people.

Ray Mears runs an advanced survival course, where participants have to survive with only a knife and a cooking pot for three days. But they are not alone, they act as a group—and while some hunt, others forage for mushrooms, and others tend the fire.

In everyday life, however, the practical need to belong to a group in order to survive no longer exists. But other needs remain. Humans are quorum sensitive too. When we operate too much on our own, we lose something vital that can only be got from being in a certain kind of community. I hazard a guess that this kind of community should feel necessary and meaningful on several levels to the individual. There is a lot of talk about "community," but what is often promised is a level of interaction so banal and unchallenging as to make one want to laugh, or scream.

In a purely economic sense, the lone individual is now a viable unit. Lonely, but viable. We may cluster together in cities, but communities that are anything more than sleeping arrangements are increasingly rare. Quorum sensitivity, however, is a part of our hardwiring that we ignore at our peril. I think the warning signs are all around us: increasing feelings of meaninglessness, pessimism, depression, suicide.

All of these are "unintelligent" responses to loneliness. But perhaps bacteria and great auks have something to teach us. These primitive organisms are "stupid" below a certain number. Maybe we too find it increasingly hard to think clearly about meaning in life when we slip below a certain number of genuine human connections, when the "real" community is not maintained.

The great auk didn't need to live in a colony of thousands to survive. It was just programmed to do that. It didn't like living in any smaller numbers. Even when the numbers were constantly being reduced by hunting, the great auk stayed put.

Psychologically, the great auk was maladjusted when it came to survival. But aren't we all a little like this?

The last great auks were killed on the islands around Saint Kilda in 1844. It seems significant to me that they died out in such a desolate spot, a place where men eventually chose not to live.

I had been in deserted villages in the Pyrenees, just over the border from where Père David was born. To come down to a deserted village in spring sunshine is a disturbing experience. The little roofs catch the light, and from a distance things look normal. Even a dog can be heard barking. But as you approach you see the holes in the roofs, the absence of glass—only a rimey ridge of hoarfrost in a window frame. And the barking dog is wild, thin as a wolf and endlessly circling the decayed houses. No one wants to stay around such a place.

YELLOW JUMPER

M Y WIFE reminded me that I now had a wife and child to support, so there could be no question of giving up and returning the advance. The following month she was taking our son to Egypt to visit his grandparents, and someone had to pay for the flight. She even offered to write the book herself if necessary, or at least type it up from my rough notes.

On the same day she winkled out of me that I had, in my indecent haste to leave Woburn, left behind in a drawer in the guest wing a rather fine, not inexpensive canary-yellow sleeveless sweater. My wife told me to ring up the housekeeper and ask her to send it back. For some reason I kept putting this simple task off. I didn't want to get in touch with Woburn again. Though it was a really nice canary yellow. And sleeveless sweaters are my favorite sweaters.

Other things I had "lost" were remembered and served as evidence against me: the boat I'd bought, which was last heard of in a boatyard that was demolished to make way for the Millennium Dome; the computer I had abandoned when I took a dislike to the irremovable margins on the desktop page. Crimes of responsibility, only of relevance to marriage.

The lost yellow jumper became a symbol of the project—there for the taking, but ignored, heedlessly cast aside.

Paranoid imaginings started to cloud my decision-making mind. What if the Chinese had been tipped off by Maja Boyd that I was a dodgy character, not to be trusted? I could be apprehended at the airport and bundled into an interrogation center, cross-examined about my belief in the significance of the McDonald's in Tiananmen Square. Even my interest in deer could be treated as suspect—what if I was there to infect them with a killer virus? Maybe I would be onto the pandas next. Spending time with the Major had given me a guilty conscience.

China, the yellow jumper—I was getting careless.

EXTINCTION III

WE KNOW we are at risk, living, as we do, in a time when the extinction of life on this planet is a widely held possibility.

Yet knowing this does not always help us, since there is also a widespread feeling that "nothing can be done."

To avoid this paralysis, one must understand that what is possible is not the extinction of the human race in the way that the Polynesian snails became extinct—precisely, on the dot—but extinction great-auk style—bit by bit, individual by individual, without us really reacting.

It starts with how we think, this endless inner landscape of ours, laid out in our minds, vast cities of cogniscence and sentience. And inside our heads, don't cities fight against cities? And as we fly over our inner domain, don't different personalities compete for the pilot's seat, and don't we, in the end, conclude that the controls are mostly set, the door to the flight deck is locked?

The twentieth century saw a vast increase in the complexity of what it means to be an individual. We have become mysteries to ourselves, containing within us a secret civilization, until now hardly suspected.

No wonder man calls himself proudly a survivor. Having survived the shrinking of his outside world and the stripping away of his traditional tools of life determination, he is, at the same time, having to survive the exploitation of his inner world by those who would control his moods, states, desires, promoting greed to obscure his real needs.

The plane flies in low, swooping haphazardly over cities at night, lights and buildings and roads twinkling as far as the eye can see. The observing self flies in and knows that once it lands, it too will become only part of this vast inner landscape. Lost in whatever part of the mind it finds itself in.

And the inner landscape remains alive because we are flying over it. If we remain on the ground too long, then it starts to die. If we stop being able to take a step back from things, we begin to die.

Shopping malls and cars and widescreen television are all very well, but in many ways they are totally unnecessary veils that encourage us to sleep and forget we are human beings put on this planet in order to gain some wisdom about life. And it's not even the number of things we own that's important, it's our relationship to them, how much they own us rather than we owning them.

Every group suffers from "the desire to persist in itself." Our society is no different, it persists through economic growth. Even if individuals are quite happy with life, there is a need for expansion in modern society, just as there was an innate need for war in most ancient societies. Further expansion is most easily fueled by individuals becoming extinct.

In many ways the individual is more at risk now than he has ever been. His ability to think is overwhelmed by useless noise. He is encouraged to become a passive consumer, supporter, viewer. He has to go outside the mainstream to find opportunities for his inner powers of self-reliance to develop.

Hope, self-belief, natural wonder: all these can be switched off, year by year, and slowly the individual becomes extinct. The lights in those vast cities grow dim, flicker, go out, plunging the inner world into a paralyzing darkness.

An extinct individual will consume, party, work, and die—all that the modern world requires of him—and he will do it willingly. The unwilling ones can be persuaded with further economically useful products such as tranquilizers, antidepressants, sleeping pills, recreational drugs, television.

And there *is* something phony in our concern for animals. We distract ourselves by worrying about animals, yet continue blindly to trample wherever the money, the goods, the lifestyle take us.

If a human skill is lost forever, isn't that just as sad as losing a type of insect or a variety of plant? If truths about humanity are killed off, isn't that worse than losing your country's population of deer?

If sanity is lost, or the conditions that make sanity possible start to disappear, aren't we then beginning to lose everything?

I remember that footage of Chernobyl, years later, deer and foxes in a kind of Eden, an insane Eden of our making.

All along it is not animals that have been most at risk, but ourselves, our innermost selves.

DIVINATION

THE DUCHESS of Bedford's single-engined airplane was reported lost off the coast of East Anglia, March 1937.

The sailors' reading room was alive with the news of it, swaying with sea legs, as the sun came through the windows all round in a circle and the wooden-shoed sailors tip-tapped from *Lloyd's List* to the public house serving Adnams ale in jugs.

Down at the beach, farther from where the farmers plowed to the low mud cliffs, the sea foamed in and out, curtains of water, well behaved and on the flat, drawing themselves across sands pocked only with lugworm holes and their mysterious hierophantic castings.

Down to a sea of low gaseousness, a sea that will toe the line. The same sea that, behind our backs, has cast Dunwich in a slow arc over its cliff, and thrown ashore, like the femur of some strange mechanical beast, a bone for the scryer to work with, the wooden strut of a crashed airplane.

The Duke of Bedford would outlast his wife by three years. The war that was about to be fought, he would never know how that would end, and his son a pacifist too.

Seas building in the turbulent channels off Dogger Bank. Cold green water sluicing off the decks of trawlers. Seas rising to no call but their own. Waves stooping in the almost feathered hardness of barrels. A stream of water dripping with purpose from the exhaust of a crab boat's engine inside the battered harbor. Surf booming against the head wall and, miraculously still, a sun.

But that now is gone. A preternatural darkness of teatime thundery cloud spreads across the canvas, drawing in the limits, pinching the horizon with rain.

Rain moving like pestilence across the sullen, cat's-pawed sea that holds its breath, strains against the leash.

There is a wind now, got up at last, coming off the pine woods on the cliffs, bending the leaning trees like palms in a hurricane.

Sea and sky are one. You know now why they say a filthy day. Dirty weather is like a spillage of gray-black ink. Sucking up the surface of the sea into a thing without humor or reason.

You hear that lack of reason in the halyards beating the mast, again and again, ropes clattered by the mad fingers of the wind, whipping the pitch-pine spars with an unanswerable rhythm.

Seas mounting in protest, unwilling almost in their violence, known now by their land-mine bombing of the front, making walking out well nigh impossible.

And out farther, where the last silly boat is making dead progress, running on bare poles and trailing a mile of oily warps, out in places where the land does not figure—five miles or five hundred from the cozy coastline hamlet, in these places where the dull plates of water slide over the surface of tormented shoulders, where gray and green disappear into the wide vigilance of men whose survival is a freak, where the surface now is all afire with white as if the undersides of the sea are stung repeatedly . . .

There would be no wreckage except a wing strut of her tiny yellow plane, washed up on the pebbly beach.

The clock chains are wound in the longcase clocks. The atonement atones. Even now the atonement atones. Ringing through the hours as the time is adjusted. One by one the lamps are removed from the curtained windows. All now is quiet in the safe cottages along the wet road of the seafront.

REASONS II

ON THE Internet I found a very cheap ticket to Beijing. I told myself it was a sign that I should go. A friend of my wife's was coming to stay and the visit would overlap with my China trip. This meant I didn't feel too bad about leaving. So I went.

As I was on an extreme budget I checked into the Sea Star Hotel—a real backpackers' dive with a dormitory. For an extra 100 yuan a night I got my own "room," which was a fenced-in cubicle fashioned from fiberboard with a low metal bed taking up the floor space.

The hotel was mercifully overheated. Everywhere else was dry, windy, and very cold.

I put a call through to Maja Boyd, who seemed to be living at a kind of guest house for foreigners. The man on the desk spoke about three words of English but took my number.

Wearing several jerseys and a cagoule, I hired a bike—which was huge and had barely functional rod brakes—costing less per day than a Beijing Big Mac. Using my hated Lonely Planet map, I headed out to Morrison Street, because it's always better to see things you have a connection to, however slight, than to rely on seeing the normal sites. Now called Wangfujing Street, it has to be the wealthiest, most Westernized street in Beijing. Even bicycles are banned in favor of traffic. In the eighties it was known briefly as McDonald's Street because of an early outpost of junk food, now torn down to build yet another mall. Morrison always believed that China's future lay in Westernization, so it seems appropriate that "his" street should have become this monstrous row of shops.

Chaining my bicycle up using the child's combination lock supplied by the hire company, I explored the Forbidden City. Somehow I thought it would be much bigger—it certainly looks smaller than it does in the film *The Last Emperor*. One thing you notice is how thick the walls are. Most memorable for me was the well down which the dowager empress threw the Pearl Concubine when she was making her exit from Peking as the Boxer Rebellion ended. This extreme act was prompted, according to some sources, by the Pearl Concubine wanting to accompany the young emperor against the dowager's wishes. The well, situated incongruously in a courtyard next to the Hall of Pleasure and Longevity, was so small I found it hard to believe the Pearl Concubine wouldn't have got stuck halfway down. Needless to say, the original version of this story can be traced back to Backhouse. The Chinese have erected a sign near the well attesting to the fate of the Pearl Concubine, turning another story into history.

I also visited the Hall of Clocks and Watches inside the larger Hall of Preserving Harmony. Most of the clocks are nineteenth-century European and Japanese. One is a kitsch lighthouse clock, late nineteenth century, which had been a great favorite of the dowager empress.

After several cold, bright days of fun-packed tourism and good conversations with freaky foreigners in the Sea Star Hotel, I was really beginning to enjoy myself. My confidence was returning. I called the bazooka range but it was shut for repairs. The Nan Haizi Deer Reserve never answered the phone, so eventually I took an expensive cab there.

It is possible to see Milu through the slats in a gate in the eight-foot wall, and not surprisingly they look just the same as the ones in Woburn, not even thinner and mangier, which is what I had been anticipating.

After flashing my Oxford University Bodleian Library card and a lot of waiting a dusty, cold waiting room, I was ushered in to meet Milu's keeper, Mr. Fu. He wore steel-rimmed glasses and chain-smoked 555-brand cigarettes.

Mr. Fu was pleased to see me and keen to speak to me as an equal in the field of deer management. He seemed to think Maja Boyd was in Japan. On the subject of the Dukes of Bedford, he had nothing but praise. Such men, he implied, were the hope of any nation. As for the Cultural Revolution, he said, looking at me meaningfully, "No good, no good."

Mr. Fu wore a tie, and when we strolled out to look at Milu he had a blue boilersuited underling open gates for us and hold a bucket of fodder under one deer's nose.

The climate in China suits Milu better than the United Kingdom. They lose fewer through the disease MCF (malignant catarrhal fever) than in the United Kingdom, Mr. Fu explained. He then went on at length about the genetic weaknesses in the world stock. "All from one," he said, holding up his finger. "All from one." The genetic weaknesses meant that Pere Davids produced fewer surviving offspring than other deer and were more sensitive to diseases like MCF. Mr. Fu thought that sensitivity to disease was increasing.

Milu can breed with red deer, producing a hybrid more robust than a pure Pere David. "But then where is Milu?" asked Mr. Fu.

He took me to see the remains of the original wall of Nan Haizi. It is a section about four hundred yards long and about twenty feet high, with sloping sides like a sea wall. We walked through a collapsed part, mud and stones on the ground, just like in Père David's day.

"How long can Milu survive with these genetic weaknesses then?" I asked.

"No one know," said Mr. Fu. "But I think longer than me and you!"

HAPPY ENDING

A STORY WITH a happy ending is somehow less scientific than a tragic extinction. Pondering why something became extinct seems more precise, scientifically speaking, than celebrating something that didn't quite die out.

Superficially, tragedy seems to have more truth in it than comedy. A long face equals serious science. But the truth in tragedy, though a warning, takes something vital away from us. The truth in comedy doesn't do this.

I'd always assumed the Novelist's novel would have an unhappy ending. Somehow that fitted in with his no-nonsense atheistic (I imagined) image. One day in the pub where they play no music, as I was slopping his pint of ale down in front of him, I asked him point-blank.

"It does, actually," he said.

"But how can a dark novel called *The Dark* have a happy ending?"

He sipped at the salivalike froth on his beer. "Why not?"

SPARROWS

FOR THE first time I notice some sparrows in the garden. When we first came here I am sure there were none. Now there are several. Maybe the sparrows are coming back.

EZBEKIYA GARDENS

THE EZBEKIYA *Gardens book market had, as far as I could work out, been destroyed in 1991. I wasn't surprised. It tied in with how the nineties saw the final triumph of globalism. Now there really is no place to hide. The wild places are just waste grounds now, interesting enough as places to play if you are a child, or in need of a holiday. They don't function as wild places anymore, not unless you are careless and forget your radio beacon and satellite phone.*

This used to make me angry and sad, but then I convinced myself it didn't matter that much. I had long nurtured this idea that things like secondhand books were overlooked by "progress" because they didn't get in the way. The old could, in this situation, happily coexist alongside the new. The death of Ezbekiya Gardens proved how wrong I was. It was the last straw. Not only had an idyllic place where people could go for a evening stroll been destroyed, so had a storehouse of knowledge. Now *Ezbekiya Gardens* was a traffic intersection with human passersby, a scene from a flyover, a brief glimpse of concrete, then gone. But the books disappearing, that was worse. That was a strike to the heart.

Nadim agreed to take me around Khan al Kalil bazaar. He went there often with his wife, who loved to bargain.

Nadim was a Catholic, he wasn't fasting, but out of consideration for me he didn't suggest a cup of tea or coffee.

First we went looking for old tools, since I had decided to give up more or less on the hunt for secondhand books. We found several junk shops in Mosky Alley, but the tools were overpriced and so worn as to be useless. Egypt is not a good place for antiques. Things get used until they wear out and break. There isn't the same reverence for old objects that we show.

Nadim then took me to a man who sold ivory. The man spoke good English and wore elliptical-lensed spectacles like a French intellectual. His shop was on the main alley in Khan al Kalil, so he must have been making money. He showed his camel-bone carvings in the front of the shop and the ivory carvings in the back. He didn't mind that we were not interested. Unlike most bazaaris, this man was not greedy. Nadim asked him about secondhand tools and he told us about a shop that specialized in them. He also gave us a map to find a place that sold swordsticks, which are still legal in Egypt.

The ivory man was helpful; he could see beyond the end of his nose. Most people in the bazaar were not like that. They didn't believe people would come back, or they didn't believe correct or considerate behavior would bring repeat custom. The majority view was get the money and screw the customer because you'll never see him again.

We looked at some swordsticks and I bargained for one that was made from *an old fencing foil set into an ebony handle. We reached an impasse and the man said, "It's only ten pounds we're arguing about, that's nothing, pay my price!"*

"If it's nothing, why not accept my price?" I said.

The man laughed and acknowledged my verbal victory, but he still wouldn't drop his price.

Nadim had been very useful, so I asked him if he knew about the move from Ezbekiya Gardens to Hussain, which was near to where we now were.

"Why don't we ask?" he said.

In the first shop we went into, a man was selling religious tracts. He told Nadim, "They came here, the booksellers, but now they've gone back. They are back in Ezbekiya Gardens."

"Are you sure?" Nadim said.

The man shrugged, as if to say, If you don't believe me, then that's your problem; you asked me and I told you.

I told my wife that Ezbekiya Gardens was maybe running again. I found even the possibility incredibly heartening. I was like a man who had lost faith and then miraculously found it again.

If the secondhand book market still existed, it meant far more than just being able to buy cheap first editions of Victor Hugo. It meant that something I cared for had not become extinct.

The great auk, the passenger pigeon, the dodo, that snail from the Pacific, those fish the Major poisoned—I had to admit that my concern for them was virtually nil. My concern was simply the result of a conventional upbringing, nothing more. Even the fact that Milu had survived rather than been killed by the hungry relief battalions, including a starving Grandpa Tom, meant little more to me than a good yarn; the deer did, of course, look nice at Woburn, but care? Really care? About a few animals, when the WORLD was disappearing?

But if Ezbekiya Gardens had somehow re-formed or continued, then I would have to change my views. Cynicism, nihilism, and global self-death predictions would be wrong. It wasn't just that Ezbekiya Gardens stood for something I cared about, secondhand books; it was the whole idea of a market for secondhand books as a conduit to the past for things of value.

Things of value. It is not antiques that are valuable, it is the workmanship, which indicates a higher level of skill and dedication than we have today. It is what the antiques can teach us that is important, not their scarcity or price.

And books are one of the best possible ways of preserving what is valuable, what should be passed on. So the book market becomes a symbol for the passing on, the willingness to pass on the ancient knowledge of the past.

My wife agreed to come with me to look for the revived Ezbekiya Gardens. We stopped in a crowded street, and the driver, Yusuf, asked a fruit-seller where the secondhand book market was. The man said there wasn't one. My wife wanted to give up, but I knew that we had to push on. We wandered around asking everyone we met. One man told us to try over there, and pointed down a wide alley to a newly paved pedestrianized piazza-type place. It was full of single-story brick-built kiosks with roll-down metal shutters. Most of the shutters were open—revealing—books!

I took in the sight at once. There must have been at least a hundred different places selling secondhand books. I did a low pass, quickly scanning the teetering piles—many were foreign-language books. Many textbooks, but many other kinds of books too. In one shop I bought a first edition of Somerset Maugham's essays, in another, a 1948 edition of Men Only with an article by Alan Whicker, and a pirated edition of Anthony Burgess—total cost three pounds sterling. In another shop the keen owner showed me his "old" books—tatty leather-bound volumes of Punch and a damaged first edition of Burton's First

Footsteps in East Africa. *He was very proud of his shop. He told us the stallholders had built all the kiosks themselves, after they had received permission to return. They had indeed been exiled for a while to Hussain, but all along they had been working at coming back to Ezbekiya Gardens. There were so many bookshops I could only skip through the mounds of books very quickly. I'd need hours to go through them properly. A lot of junk, but far more variety than in an English secondhand book market. Here there was more room for surprises. There were French, German, Italian, Russian books—relics of the various times when those countries had sought to influence Egypt. Ezbekiya Gardens was back in force. I even found a first edition of Victor Hugo. It was as if it had been waiting ever since Nadim and his brother had shopped there, a companion volume, still remarkably cheap. Old books with pictures commanded a premium as they do in the West, and the condition of most of the books was not perfect. But Egypt is a dry country, and the books had no worm or mildew, which is the problem in wetter places.*

If the booksellers could survive in the hostile commercial environment of Egypt, I felt they could survive anywhere. In a place where "influence" is a standard procedure to gain building permission, a place where previously beautiful areas have been ruined by high-rise blocks of incredible ugliness, where demands for housing mean that slum dwellings eat into the fields around Cairo, it was remarkable that the booksellers had clung onto their home turf. In Egypt, the ancient bangs right up against the modern, people living in tombs in the City of the Dead and talking on mobile phones. The pressure to modernize is intense, yet somehow the ability to be individual has not been crushed. The booksellers remain.

Milu survives. If you visit Woburn Abbey or Whipsnade Zoo, you can see examples of this strange ungulate that has survived against all odds, and largely because of the efforts of two extraordinary men. Or not so extraordinary. I rather think they were ordinary men who knew when to make an extraordinary effort. Ordinary men, like the booksellers of Ezbekiya Gardens.

EPILOGUE

GRANDPA TOM'S wooden writing box, long thought to be lost, turned up mysteriously in the post, sent by a cousin who had heard I was researching the Boxer Rebellion. Tom's medals, in envelopes long since opened, still had iridescent silk ribbons that looked as if they had been made that day.

The Novelist's novel was published to huge acclaim, winning prizes both here and in the United States. It was indeed his breakthrough novel.

In a most dramatic turn of events, the Major was wounded in a shoot-out in the London Library, having taken A. S. Byatt hostage in the stacks. She was miraculously unharmed after a heroic "swap" was made with a red-coated library flunkey. The red-coat was an armed policeman in disguise, who shot the Major at point-blank range. The Major is currently under armed guard at the Cromwell Hospital, awaiting extradition to Australia on charges of marsupial genocide.

Months later, and unasked, Lord Howland's housekeeper sent the yellow jumper back.